THE GIFTS OF
AUTISM & ALZHEIMER'S

Stories of Unconditional Love & Self-Determination

KEN ROUTSON & NANCY REDER RN

THE GIFTS OF AUTISM & ALZHEIMER'S

Stories of Unconditional Love & Self-Determination

© 2013 Ken Routson & Nancy Reder RN
ISBN: 978-1-891067-06-8
LCCN: 2013957417

Tulip Press
120 Highridge Court
Fairfield, OH 45014
tulip2252@aol.com

Book design: Barbara With
Cover photo: Stacy Catanzaro and Jamie Smed

TABLE OF CONTENTS

Preface by John Zeisel PhD.............................. 7

Foreword by By Raun K. Kaufman 9

1 Introduction 15

2 Stories of Unconditional Love & Self-Determination....21

3 Autistic Spectrum Disorder & Alzheimer's Disease 29

4 Individual Perspectives of Autism.........................35

5 The Gifts of Art & Music 49

6 Establishing Rapport & Cultivating an Atmosphere of
    Trust, Unconditional Love, Acceptance, &
    Self-Determination 75

7 Behavior is Language...83

8 Is Anyone In There?..93

9 Living In Joy with Less Stress & Resistance............. 103

10 Stories of the Spectrum 111

11 Living With Alzheimer's.................................. 127

12 Extraordinary Gifts 147

13 The Gifts of Services 153

Final Thoughts by Nancy Reder RN & Ken Routson......... 159

Suggested Reading & Other Resources...................... 163

ACKNOWLEDGEMENTS

Nancy and I are extremely grateful to all the individuals and families who shared their stories and expertise in making this book inspiring and enlightening. I am very appreciative of my editor, Kathy Sawyer, for her editorial gifts and especially for her enthusiasm, patience and care with my writing. I am forever grateful.

Furthermore, I extend special thanks to: Claire Stephens for her editing talents in my initial article regarding my mother; Barbara With for her patience and expertise; and Stacey Catanzaro and Jamie Smed for the artwork cover of this book.

Thank you to my mom's special friend, Sandy Picciano-Brand.

I have profound appreciation for my remarkable mentors with whom I had the privilege to correspond: John Zeisel Ph.D., Gabor Mate M.D., Peter Whitehouse M.D., Robert Melillo Ph.D., Thomas Armstrong Ph.D. and Raun Kaufman. I express my deepest of gratitude to Raun Kaufman and John Zeisel for taking time out of their busy schedules to write the foreword and preface.

Finally I want to especially express the deepest of gratitude to my beloved spiritual partner, Leslie Stewart, for her enthusiasm and assistance in this project and for her patience during my years of research and writing. I am eternally grateful for her kind and special relationship with my mother.

Nancy Reder would like to express her heartfelt thanks to her friend and editor: Lauren Seewaldt Gelbart, for her assistance with editing Nancy's contributions to this book. Lauren is a strong advocate for persons with special needs.

DEDICATION

This book is dedicated to my dear mom, Fern Eloise Routson, and to all those labeled with Autism or Dementia who are much more than their diagnosis, with more gifts than their labels suggest.

To all the caregivers whose tender loving care can never be appreciated enough.

To my beloved father, Kenneth who exemplified unconditional love.

Ken Routson

Nancy Reder dedicates this book to her granddaughters, Andreya and Anastasia. "May they live in and contribute to a world that is accepting and appreciative of differences."

She thanks Emmett, her husband "who is always supportive, encouraging, and there for me when I need him. Thank you, my best friend."

By John Zeisel PhD

I interviewed an older woman about her housing needs in a low-income Boston neighborhood years ago. She spoke about views of the street from the living room being important to her so she could watch her grandkids play, and a kitchen large enough to have her family over for holiday dinners. She was from somewhere in the south, Georgia I think it was, and had plants and vines growing abundantly in her south-facing living room window. She did not have much, yet was full of wisdom and joy.

As I was leaving, I thanked her for taking time for the interview and asked how her vines grew so well. I don't remember her exact words—something about loving her plants—but I remember clearly that while she spoke, she walked slowly to the window and snipped a cutting which she held out to me. Before I had uttered the words "Thank you," she stopped me in my tracks. "Don't ever thank anyone for a cutting" she said emphatically, as if I had committed a real faux pas. "Why"? I asked. "Because God made the plants," she said, "and the gift that cuttings continue to grow even after they are ripped from their stem has nothing to do with me. So don't say thank you to me!"

Gifts of ideas, of hope, of life belong to everyone. "The Gifts of Alzheimer's: Insights gained from learning to give and receive," chapter ten of my book *I'm Still Here*, highlights the voices of people I have known who have received such gifts—not from me, but from their lives and their pain. Like the cutting I received years ago, these are not gifts they can thank anyone for—definitely not a thank you to Dr. Alzheimer or to the Greeks for the term "autism." They are the gifts gained from passing through pain and suffering and coming out on top—or at least in equilibrium.

Zen Buddhist teacher Thich Nhat Hanh points out that lotus flowers—a symbol of wisdom, compassion, and life—only grow in the mud of shallow pools. The art of suffering is living through it; the art of suffering is not dwelling in it; the art of suffering is emergence—like a lotus flower. "No mud, no lotus."

This book is about the art of suffering—living it, not dwelling in it, coming through it. The many voices of joy, the many styles, the many expressions of love and learning all come together in a chorus of hope. Harvard Professor Marshall Ganz defines "hope" as

YCMAD—You Can Make a Difference. The gift that each voice in this book echoes is the gift of knowing that they have made a difference. The gift each voice in this book echoes is the gift of knowing that she and he has made a difference in the life of someone they love. The gift each voice in this book expresses is the joy that comes from knowing that the world is a little better because of something we did—a simple act.

Karma is the knowledge that our whole lives reverberate in response to our actions. That is what this book is about—knowing that we can make a difference and that there is hope. No "thank you" for that gift.

John Zeisel PhD is president of the I'm Still Here Foundation & Hearthstone Alzheimer Care, and author of *I'm Still Here: A New Philosophy of Alzheimer's Care*

By Raun K. Kaufman

Once you read this book, you will never be able to unread it.

And trust me, that's a good thing.

It's a good thing because it means that you will never be able to see only one side of autism, Alzheimer's, and many other seemingly tragic diagnoses and conditions. You will no longer be able to sustain the idea that these challenges can only be seen as unmitigated hardships and unsolvable conundrums. You'll have a difficult time maintaining the feelings of hopelessness so deeply embedded in our culture. You won't view fear or sadness as the only human responses to having a loved one diagnosed with autism or Alzheimer's. And it will no longer be possible for you to be able to look at someone you care about with neurological challenges and simultaneously think to yourself, "There's nothing I can do to meaningfully impact my loved one's condition."

When you finish *The Gifts of Autism and Alzheimer's*, the title, which might seem preposterous to some, will be fact for you. Of course, no one sits around wishing for their child to have autism or their parent or partner to have Alzheimer's. And this book certainly doesn't ask you to do such a thing. But once someone you love already has either of these diagnoses, this book will open your eyes to see the gifts and the possibilities within that person's challenges—and in so doing, to be maximally helpful to that person.

And, hey, I'm not just some guy pontificating about a subject of academic or professional interest. I'm someone who has been there and back.

I fully recovered from severe autism.

When I was a young boy, I was diagnosed as severely autistic, with a tested I.Q. of less than 30. I didn't respond to my name or any other attempts at communication. I made no eye contact with others. I was mute, with no language or any verbal indication of wants whatsoever. I seemed completely shut off to the world, often appearing to be deaf. Although I displayed no interest in other people, I remained fascinated with inanimate objects, such as kitchen plates. In fact, I would often sit on the floor and spin a kitchen plate on its edge for hours and hours on end. Other repetitive behaviors (called "stims" by most in the autism community), such as rocking back and forth or flapping my hands in front of my face, would continue throughout each day. I didn't want to be held and would often recoil from human touch.

After receiving a diagnosis of severe autism, my parents raced from specialist to specialist, trying to find solutions. Instead, they received only the grimmest of prognoses.

I would be severely autistic for the rest of my life. I would never speak, certainly not in sentences. I would never have the capability to make friends and form meaningful relationships. I would always prefer objects to people.

And the predictions mounted. I would never go to a regular school, have a girlfriend or a job, a first love or a last day of summer camp. For me, there would be no high school or college graduation, no buying my first car or moving into my first home, no career.

I would, always and forever, be encapsulated within my own world. The recommendation: eventual lifelong institutionalization.

The only reason that this future did not become my future was because my parents (authors and teachers Barry Neil Kaufman and Samahria Lyte Kaufman) made a deliberate decision to see my autism as a gift, not a curse; an opportunity, not a calamity. Discarding the pessimism and behavior-modification focus of traditional autism treatment, my parents developed a program to reach me. They called it The Son-Rise Program®.

Rather than trying to force me to conform to a world that I did not yet understand, they began by joining me in my world. This led to the development of the first signature technique of The Son-Rise Program®: joining. When I would spin a plate, my mother would get a plate of her own and spin with me. When I would rock back and forth, my mother would rock with me.

Although many professionals vociferously criticized my parents at the time, they proved incredibly prescient. As they joined me, I began to trust them, bond with them, and let them into my world. For the first time, I started looking at them and smiling at them. They were valuing my world, my experience, my differentness, my interests, and, yes, my autism!

As I let them in, they encouraged me to come out, inviting me to engage with them, communicate with them, and play with them. They slowly built up my social interaction by designing games and activities centered around interests and motivations that I already had, such as animals and airplanes.

After working with me every day for three and a half years, I emerged from my autism without any trace of my former condition. All of those futures that I was never supposed to have—friends, girlfriends, first loves and last days of summer camp, sports teams, graduating college (I graduated from Brown University with a degree in Biomedical Ethics), a fulfilling career—I went on to experience all of them.

After my recovery, my father recounted our story in the bestselling book *Son-Rise: The Miracle Continues*, which was made into an award-winning NBC-TV movie called *Son-Rise: A Miracle of Love*. In 1983, my parents founded the Autism Treatment Center of America(tm), part of a charitable non-profit organization in the Berkshire Mountains of Sheffield, Massachusetts. The ATCA serves as the worldwide teaching center for The Son-Rise Program®. Parents and professionals come from all over the world for week-long training programs so that they can help their children in a loving, respectful, and open-hearted way to grow beyond their original prognoses.

As for my role, I am the former CEO and current Director of Global Education at the ATCA, and I've spent the past fifteen years working to get the techniques of The Son-Rise Program® into the hands of families who can use them, whether by helping families individually, working with professionals, conducting lectures and seminars throughout Europe and the United States or, most recently, writing my book *Autism Breakthrough: The Groundbreaking Method That Has Helped Families All Over the World*.

I know that it is the ending to my story that captures people's imaginations (and, needless to say, I'm very happy with the outcome!), but it is so crucial to understand that the most important part of the story—especially as you read this book—is the beginning of the story. My parents began by seeing the gifts in my autism—before I had changed one iota. They looked at me with wonder, not fear or sadness. They saw possibilities, not deficiencies.

This is what Ken Routson invites us to do in this book! Just as this vantage point gave my parents a way in with me, it will give you a way in with your loved one!

And, like me, Ken's been through his own special experiences. Born with speech aphasia and other profound learning disabilities, Ken has befriended and overcome his challenges. He has also had an amazing journey with his own mother with Alzheimer's, which I will let him tell you himself.

Because he is the sort of person who is not only smart, creative, and passionate, but is also very giving with a big heart, Ken has spent the past forty years reaching out to help others with challenges. He has collected a host of well-deserved national awards and recognitions for his work and has engaged in such meaningful projects as developing and coordinating a foster care program and pioneering some of the very first supported living programs in Ohio. He has devoted himself to helping people with severe challenges to grow, develop, and live more empowered and independent lives. He conducts life coaching seminars, sensitivity training workshops, and lectures, which serve as a testament to his triumph over adversity and desire to help others to do the same.

Unlike most, Ken really "gets" people with autism and Alzheimer's. He really understands what makes people with either of these challenges tick—and what gets their way. If you are not familiar with Ken's work, I think you will be very pleasantly surprised by the useful knowledge that he brings to the table.

(You may be wondering why in the world he's putting these two seemingly disparate challenges together in the same book. They're not as unrelated as you might think! After reading Ken's words, you will see that the principles of helping these two groups of people can be incredibly similar—and so are the gifts and wisdom they have for us!)

Ken appreciates the absolute importance of establishing rapport and cultivating an atmosphere of trust, unconditional love, acceptance, and self-determination. (Hey, wait a minute, that's the title of Chapter 6!) In my work, I've seen very little that's as essential.

Ken recognizes how crucial attitudes and emotions are for those who are able to be of help to people with autism or Alzheimer's. People with these challenges—*because* of these challenges—are very attuned to the emotions and attitudes of the people caring for them. (Ken doesn't overlook the huge impact that our attitudes and emotions can have on our own health, as well.) Ken's discussion of this issue is so vital because I very often hear fear, anger, sadness or frustration disguised as humanity or compassion. Ken gets that feeling bad—even if we feel bad for someone—is not the same as loving and caring for someone.

Ken's real grasp of the experiences of people with various challenges leads him to be able to effectively explain the significance of creating a safe and loving environment—and how to do that.

I remember reading about Ken's experience years ago when he would drive challenged children to school, and he saw that if he played the right kind of music, the children would rock themselves and be calmed over the course of the drive. He was very excited—until he received a call from the special education director about concerns voiced by other teachers that Ken was encouraging this self-soothing and thereby reinforcing "socially-unacceptable behavior." Although I have no doubt that the director and the other teachers had good intentions, this kind of total misunderstanding and undervaluing of these kids' experiences leads to extremely unhelpful, counterproductive, and ultimately unkind ways of dealing with them. I know how critical Ken's book is because such undermining mindsets still dominate.

And this is even truer for people with Alzheimer's. Ken recounts a story of a staff member at an assisted-living facility taking away the doll that his mother, Fern, was holding (like a baby) in order to give Fern her medicine. The staff member told Fern that she could not have the doll back until she took her medicine. (It probably goes without saying that this proposition did not go down well!)

This takes us to a fundamental concept that we teach at the ATCA and that Ken gets across in a deep way: the importance of focusing on the relationship rather than behavior change. So often, we try to bludgeon others—including those we love most—into behaving the way we want them to. Though we may have the best of reasons, in the end we are prioritizing behavior modification over relationship creation (and preservation). We are placing compliance above connection. In essence, we are valuing what the person does on the outside more than their experience on the inside. This is especially ironic since, when it comes to those we love, often times our stated reasons for pushing, pulling, and getting frustrated are that this person we love "needs" to do X in order to be okay, to succeed, be treated well by the world, and, ultimately, have a good life experience. In our strenuous efforts to give those we love with autism, Alzheimer's or other neurological challenges an imagined better life experience tomorrow, we violate, destabilize, and upset their life experience today. Isn't that strange?

I could go on and on about the efficacy and overall awesomeness of what Ken delves into in this book, but that's his job! And he does it well! Ken provides solutions that are pragmatic in implementation yet revolutionary in outlook and repercussions.

Additionally, Ken proposes wild and fun conceptual frameworks, such as the possibility of an inner dimension of consciousness analogous to the World Wide Web where all previous knowledge and wisdom exists—and which he playfully calls the "inner-net." Ha! One of the many wonderful things about Ken as an author is that he doesn't demand that you adopt his novel, outside-the-box perspectives; he simply invites you to play with the ideas. In so doing, he gives you the opportunity to open your mind and expand your viewpoint—not for the sake of some abstract enlightenment but so that you can approach those you love who face challenges such as autism and Alzheimer's with an open heart and an outstretched hand. This is something that we at the ATCA teach parents and is the key jumping-off point to providing real, meaningful help.

This book is a spectacular marriage of psychology and physiology; of attitude/emotion and biology. It is filled with critically important perspectives to adopt, practical advice on putting those beliefs into action, and remarkable examples. In fact, one of the most moving and indispensable aspects of this book is the beautiful collection of chapters written first-person by the touching and astute contributors. You will get so much from these people! Really take your time reading what they're written. They bring an honesty and a wisdom that will stay with you.

And, finally, I want to highlight Nancy Reder. Her fifty years of experience in medicine and disability services—working with children and adults—lends a heft and depth to this book that I think you will really appreciate.

And so I leave you, dear reader, with the great anticipation that comes from my knowing that something magnificent is in store for you! This book will help you. This book will help someone you cherish. I am so excited for you! I give enormous thanks to Ken and Nancy for making this book happen, and I feel certain that, once you finish it, you will want to do the same!

CHAPTER 1

Introduction

For over 40 years, I have worked as a consultant, CEO, and front-line staff member in an educational, medical, transportation and residential capacity, and I have had the privilege of being a partnering change agent in the field of disabilities. Our field has evolved from being controlling and dismissive of the preferences of the individuals we serve to being more person-centered and empowering for the individual.

I have asked Nancy Reder to co-author this book. Nancy is a retired RN who co-presented workshops with me in the 1980s. She has 32 years of experience with persons with special needs and a background in geriatric nursing caring for persons with Alzheimer's disease.

While observing the Alzheimer's journey of my own mother, I saw some similarities in the characteristics of those with autism and those with Alzheimer's.

The time I spent with my mom while she was at home, in assisted living, and in nursing homes culminated in my fervent desire to explore the lives of people with Alzheimer's and autism and on their effects on their families and on the community.

This book is based on my informal research as a worker in the field of disabilities and as a son caring for an affected parent: *The Gifts of Alzheimer's and Autism: Unconditional Love and Self Determination.*

Nancy and I have asked people to share their stories in our book. I emailed potential contributors the article I wrote about my mother's Alzheimer's that inspired this book.

This book is intended for parents whose children have just been given an autistic diagnosis and for families and loved ones of those with Alzheimer's. But we believe others can benefit from it as well: perhaps you are on the autism spectrum or have been given the Alzheimer's diagnosis yourself. Maybe you are a teacher, a nurse, or a dedicated employee in an assisted living or nursing home. Maybe you just like inspirational stories or are on a quest to discover your life's purpose!

Life is about relationships. Life is about change and learning how to go with the flow with ease and joy instead of with resistance, stress, fear, and despair. Relationships are about connecting, compromising, receiving, sharing, giving, and communicating.

This book is about the power and value of unconditional love, music, theater, art, and self-determination. It is about the power and love of God, life, the universe, faith, patience, solitude, trust, prayer, meditation, and nature.

It is our desire that you will be inspired and uplifted by all of the inspirational stories of love, tears, joy, pain, humor, self-determination, and human compassion.

Sadly, much fear, trauma, horror, and despair are associated with the two conditions which are the focus of this book. With the recent increase of autism and Alzheimer's, it is safe to say that most people will have a friend or family member with one of these challenges (or they themselves are faced with one of them) during some point in their lives. We have chosen to focus on helping others to make peace with whatever challenge they inherit or develop and to find some positive aspects of it.

There is definitely no shortage of books on the anguish and despair and fear surrounding autism and Alzheimer's. Conversely, our book invites you to embark on your own spiritual journey, a quest, an adventure for self-discovery and for excavating some of your most hidden fears, feelings, desires, or resentments. Moreover, we invite you to discover your unknown inner strength, courage, faith, trust, love, equanimity, passion, and dauntless joy!

> God grant me the serenity to accept the things I cannot change, courage to change the things I can, and wisdom to know the difference.
>
> – Reinhold Niebuhr

This book is about learning how to trust life and about connecting with a higher power when dealing with undesirable circumstances. I believe that life is always for us if we get out of our own way. Life is meant to be good.

What can we learn from autism and Alzheimer's? Autism can teach you how to trust and let go when you need to, for example, when you are that anxious parent sending a child to school or to live on his or her own in a group home, in a supported living arrangement, or on their own independently. For parents of children with autism, there can be dignity in some risk, in the ability to allow their children to take steps toward independence.

Similarly, Alzheimer's can teach you how to let go when you are required to become your parent's caretaker as you send him or her off to a day care center or to a residential arrangement.

The eternal lesson for all of us is to trust the processes of "letting go" and of death for not only our loved ones, but also for ourselves.

I believe most of us—especially in the western world—are afraid of death. Consequently, I believe for some, the long good-bye process of death may actually be a gift for anyone who is themselves afraid to die or afraid of relinquishing the emotional holds on loved ones with Alzheimer's. As far back as I can remember, even as a small child, I had an irrational fear of my mother dying, perhaps because she was more protective of me than she was of my siblings because of her difficult pregnancy. She had lost children before through miscarriage, and the doctor warned her either that she may lose me or that I could be disabled. Fortunately, I was born with only minor learning disabilities, aphasia, and speech challenges. Finally, after receiving speech therapy, I was able to communicate better (except for occasional aphasia episodes). It is ironic to me that for much of my career I was paid to conduct workshops and seminars nationwide using the one skill that was my childhood limitation. (However, I began noticing in my late 50s that my aphasia and short attention span are sometimes more pronounced.)

I believe that because my mother was so afraid of losing me, I picked up some of this anxiety, even in utero. I believe that because of her profound fear and my own sensitivity, we developed a kind of mutual separation anxiety. However, my fear of death has greatly reduced during the spiritual introspection and growth of my adulthood. I have learned and accepted that when we let go and trust, God and life give us opportunities to love and fulfill ourselves and others.

Sometimes unexpected events and circumstances require that we delve deep within to realize how powerful we are when we consciously connect to our inner divine partnership with God. I have learned from my spiritual lessons that we get what we focus on, so it is important to sift through your current life for everything you have to be thankful for.

When I find myself in a challenging situation, I affirm to myself that everything always works out for me. When you focus on the positive aspects of your life or of the situation and let go of the negative, your life or the situation will improve. Change the way you look at things and the things you look at will change. Consequently, it is imperative to maintain a positive attitude!

When I finally made peace with the physical disappearance of my pre-Alzheimer's mom, I became receptive to embarking on a new magical relationship and journey with my "new mom." I consciously shifted my awareness to the positive aspects of "new mom." In many ways, my mother was more relaxed, not worried, at peace, and at times in bliss! There were those occasional "sundowners"—times of agitation—but for the most part, she was a much happier person. My new-found relationship with my mother inspired me to write this book.

Finally, this book is also about the power of love and the importance of establishing trusting, empowering and positive interactions and environments for our loved ones with autism and Alzheimer's. By applying these concepts and techniques with the goal of empowerment in mind, I helped facilitate many success stories for individuals with severe behavioral disabilities, many of whom had autism, and many of whom were restrained most of the time to prevent self-injurious, life-threatening behaviors. Using a common sense approach and by establishing trust and rapport with these individuals, I observed a reduction in their adverse behaviors, and in some cases, the elimination of certain behaviors.

These successes prove that there is much strength in gentleness, unconditional love and acceptance, and valuing all beings just because they exist.

Whether the individual with Alzheimer's is you yourself, or whether your loved one has Alzheimer's or autism, it is of utmost importance that you make peace with your situation. It is beneficial to release your bitterness and your negative judgments and become whole. Many who are reading this book may be playing the role of caretaker, either directly, professionally, or for a dear friend. It is imperative for the whole family or work place to maintain its wholeness! We cannot take care of others if we do not take care of ourselves. I believe that most illness is the result of self-rejection, long-term anger, chronic stress and resentments, or resisting self and life. The English word for healing originated from the German word *hailjan*, which means "to make whole." Eventually after going through either the loss of a normal child, as in the case of autism, or the shock of an Alzheimer's diagnosis, it is healing to embrace yourself and unconditionally accept and make the best of the situation. Through this book, we will be discussing the power of nurturing self and others.

As I have become what our culture calls "a senior citizen," I have realized that no matter what life brings, no matter how grim, disparaging, devastating, horrific, or gloomy, there is a broader, grander purpose, or plan, and always lessons, and sometimes even further opportunities beyond what I had realized or imagined.

As Jane Beach wrote in the March 2013 *Science of Mind* magazine:

> *Appreciation lifts us out of despair because it is impossible to be truly grateful and to be unhappy at the same time. It turns us away from what's wrong and toward what is right. We ask ourselves, "What aspect of my divine nature can I bring to this situation—peace, acceptance, love, wisdom?" The more we stay centered on the spiritual gift that is emerging within us, the more quickly the problem dissolves!*[1]

Finally, I would like to end this introductory chapter with passages from and thoughts on my favorite book about Alzheimer's, *I'm Still Here* by John Zeisel, Ph.D., beginning with the following:

> *A person living with Alzheimer's is first "a person," and only then someone with a disease. The way the world sees Alzheimer's today is that a person is almost totally lost once he or she receives an "Alzheimer's diagnosis"—lost both to themselves and to those who love them. An Alzheimer's diagnosis is seen as an Alzheimer's "sentence." But this just isn't so. Throughout the more than decade-long progress of the disease, the person is crying out, "I'm still here!" We all need to start hearing that cry before it fades away completely.*[2]

As Dr. Zeisel asserts, we must help reframe the historically fatalistic perspectives of autism and Alzheimer's and begin to provide some positive, constructive hope for those individuals and their families who must live and die with these challenges.

(Another book I highly recommend is *The Myths of Alzheimer's*, by one of the best-known Alzheimer's experts in the world, geriatric neurologist Peter Whitehouse. This book not only eliminates much of the erroneous information and propaganda surrounding Alzheimer's, but it provides a more humanistic view of the condition and encourages hope for the aging process in general.)

When I conduct sensitivity workshops throughout the country, I talk about families having to experience the loss of a normal child;

many parents who have children with autism have to adjust their expectations for their children. Similarly, I had to finally accept the loss of the relationship I used to have with my mother. As Dr. Zeisel states:

> ... he is not that person any longer. Neither can our relationships be the same. While the person still cares for us and continues to love us and we them, we must have new expectations and build a new relationship. The first step is to discard old expectations and role relationships that limit our ability to see the person and relate to him or her in a new way.[3]

May this book encourage you to focus on the abilities of the people in your life who have Alzheimer's or autism instead of the disabilities and so-called deficits—and instead value, empower, and enjoy your connection with them!

As Dr. Zeisel states:

> Love is a universal language understood far into the illness, even to the end of life. If everyone involved with the illness learns to say, 'I love you' to the other, the other person will understand and be more present, and relationships can grow."[4]

---

[1] Jane Beach, "Appreciation for What Is", *Science of the Mind*, March 2013. <http://www.scienceofmind.com/pdf/mag/2013/march/som_march_daily_guides2013.pdf>

[2] John Zeisel, *I'm Still Here: A New Philosophy of Alzheimer's Care*, (New York, NY: Penguin Group, 2010), p. 7.

[3] Ibid., p. 11.

[4] Ibid., p. 5.

CHAPTER 2

Stories of Unconditional Love & Self-Determination

The original story that follows inspired me to write this book. When I first wrote it as an article, I emailed it to potential contributors who would be willing to share their stories in a collaborative publication such as this. I wrote Part One while my mother was still alive. I wrote Part Two after her passing.

Part One
You may be saying, "Wow, this title is the epitome of an oxymoron! Gifts? Of autism? and Alzheimer's?"

Your reaction is normal for family and friends whose lives have been affected by loved ones who appear to be suffering from autism or Alzheimer's. Before I proceed, let me clarify: I am NOT saying that either condition is always a gift for the caregivers, friends, or families of those people society consider victims of disease, genetics, or various environmental factors.

During the earlier stages of my own mother's Alzheimer's, I would have been either dubious or outraged by the notion that this experience was a gift for anyone involved. I would have thought, "This is a hell of a situation, and I see no gift anywhere in sight!" I experienced the loss of my "real mom," and felt sharp emotional pain watching her kick, slap, and even bite people when she didn't get her way. I had an intense ache in my heart from the guilt I felt every time my spiritual partner, Leslie, and I drove her back to her nursing facility.

Early on in my mother's Alzheimer's journey, what first appeared to be a game of hide and seek was merely Mom hiding her purse. That started a routine—when it was time for her to go somewhere, everyone had to search for the purse. The next thing that we noticed was how she would look out her window and see children or animals that no one else could see. Leslie would show her our recent vacation pictures, and she would see animals that we could not see. Who was I to say these animals did not exist? They certainly did to her.

Then we began noticing changes in her language. The first change I witnessed was during a telephone call—which, in retrospect, was before I or anyone else suspected any form of dementia was setting in. Typically, Mom was very expressive. For several years we lived in a nearby city and I would visit her on Saturdays and call her every

Tuesday morning. Every year on my birthday, I would call her and thank her for giving birth to me and for being my mom. During my birthday call the year before, she had exhibited no signs of dementia and she cried when I thanked her. I apologized for making her sad, and she expressed herself eloquently, stating, "Quite the contrary— these are tears of joy!"

After her dementia became more apparent, however, she developed a different way of expressing herself. She would have difficulty finding the appropriate words. (Oh, how I could relate to this frustration because of my own severe learning disabilities! I still experience times of aphasia.) In the early stages of her Alzheimer's, she would express her frustration at her inability to articulate and would say, "I know what I'm saying in my head but it won't come out right."

Once, during a phone call, I sensed that she wasn't doing very well. When I asked what was wrong, she said," I feel 'dipity' when I'm upright." Like myself—with my learning disabilities—I seemed to know what she wanted to say, but she just had trouble finding the right words. For instance, during one of our last conversations I said to Leslie as she wiped my mom's mouth, "Mom said don't forget the upper level," by which she meant her upper lip.

Another morning, I walked into her assisted living room and I said, "Why are you so sad?" She responded as she gazed at her feet, "My toes are crying!"

As time passed, I came to accept my mother's odd new behaviors. As my acceptance grew, I began to notice that many of her Alzheimer's symptoms were like those of people with autism, with whom I had worked for decades.

For example, my "new mom," who previously could be controlling and anxious, could now enjoy simple things for extended periods. During our weekly rides, she would stare out the window at the clouds, study them, and describe them to us in great detail using words she had never used before: for instance when looking up and seeing vapor trails in the sky from airplanes, she would describe them as "slices."

She would comment excitedly on the beauty of objects and places we had routinely passed by for the last 20 years. She began developing relationships with inanimate objects. She seemed less anxious and more at peace with herself. She wasn't worried about anything when she was free to live according to her own schedule and not someone else's. This change was not a small one for my mother, who, as I said, spent most of her life being worried, highly anxious, impulsive, and with a tendency to try to control others, especially her children (even when her children reached adulthood). Like many mothers of her generation, she used guilt and manipulation to get the results she desired. She had always been afraid of death and did not like to be alone. However, that person is not the person I was seeing in my new mom. She is happy—not always an easy thing for others to see, but happy unto herself.

Of the very happy and contented people I have known, many of them are persons with autism. My friend Andrew would have to be at the top of this list. He has a contagious zest for life. He is enthusiastic about everything that comes into his moment-to-moment experience. Although I am certain he has times when he is unhappy or disappointed, I have yet to witness one. Even those people with autism who exhibit severe behaviors still live in the moment. My friend Addie will rapidly move from periods of great distress, which involve crying loudly and hitting herself, to fits of laughing at something, shifting herself into a much-improved state of being. Addie is easily distracted and learned to distract herself for her own benefit. Addie is very fortunate to have parents that not only love her very much but also understand that behavior is language and the importance of cultivating the living and teaching environments with valued/person-centered relationships based on unconditional love and acceptance. (See Addie's story in Chapter 10 Stories of the Spectrum that makes reference to the summer camp I developed based on philosophies discussed in this book)

As my mother's Alzheimer's has progressed, she has become more easily distractible, and therefore, less likely to spend as long appreciating things such as the clouds in the sky. However, she is still so very "in the moment," that if she is distracted, it is impossible for her to respond to something you just asked. She will be so engrossed in what now has her attention that she will totally forget the conversation she was having with you just a moment before. Basically, she savors the moment in which she finds herself. Therefore— for now anyway—unless she is agitated because of being controlled, she appears to be in a state of near perpetual bliss. For those moments when she is agitated, the best way to redirect her to an improved mood is to soothe her with her "baby"—the baby doll she believes to be real. She will rock it and sing it to sleep, sometimes falling asleep herself.

We all want to know how to live more in the moment, how to enjoy a simpler life, how to live a more blissful life, and how to discover the joy of being alive. Isn't it funny that our society spends millions of dollars on books, classes, and workshops to learn mindfulness techniques? Strange that we will spend equal amounts of time and dollars trying to stave off the disease that brings this very knowledge and experience into the center of someone's life! Society, the medical community, and families affected by Alzheimer's focus predominantly upon the negative impact (especially the challenging behaviors) of the "disabilities" that come along with Alzheimer's. I, on the other hand, am excited by the possibilities that are readily available if someone changes his or her attitude toward this "disease." The purpose of my endeavor is to suggest to families and friends of affected individuals that if they make peace with what is, they may find something rich and rewarding in what could be seen as a travesty. Until a cure is found, I've discovered that it is best to find the positive aspects in the people with such a condition.

If you are interested in this subject, you can read more now in an outstanding book by Dr. Thomas Armstrong called *Neurodiversity*.

In my book, I will consider the possible reasons and heretofore gifts of these two "diseases"—gifts which are hidden to the jaded eye. I hope my book will be of great comfort, not only to the loved ones who are living with those who have either autism or Alzheimer's, but perhaps to those with either condition as well.

I want my readers to ponder the following points:

1. The earth, with its millions of species, from plants to animals to humans, is a material mosaic of diversity; each life form is an individual expression of unique desires and purpose. Maybe there is a purpose or lesson that autism and Alzheimer's bring to humanity?

2. Life is an expanding spiritual process. By being true to itself, each member of every species will fulfill itself, thereby contributing to the fulfillment and expansion of our collective universe.

3. Society's institutions have demanded conformity at the expense of fully expressed individuals. These demands have resulted in a decrease in society in feelings of personal power, creativity, inventiveness, and imagination.

4. Society has valued and emphasized the importance of physical strength, beauty, and intelligence and has disenfranchised those who lack a certain degree of physical strength and mental ability.

I have noticed that people with autism and Alzheimer's' share a propensity for being self-directed and self-centered. I see them as able to live in the moment and have fun in the most simplistic ways. Also, for the most part, they have the ability to resist being controlled or manipulated by others. Could it be that the autistic child is not flawed? That those who acquire dementia are not flawed? Isn't it possible that they are here to serve a purpose for their spiritual evolution or society's?

Please see if the following statements ring true for you:

1. People with autism and Alzheimer's share a propensity towards being self-directed, self-centered, and in the moment and are able to have fun in the most simplistic ways. They resist being controlled or manipulated by others.

2. Persons with autism are not born with flaws, but come to serve many purposes.

3. Could Alzheimer's be nature's way of providing a natural anesthetic for those people who are afraid to die? Soothing them by taking a longer unconscious path, or what others have referred to as "the long good-bye?"

4. I'm familiar with some individuals with Alzheimer's who were once controlling, anxious, lacked self-confidence, or had a fear of the future, but as the disease progressed, they became less fearful and more able to live in and enjoy the moment.

5. If we believe that God is love and God has created a diverse Universe, then can we also believe that autism and Alzheimer's are a means to teach us unconditional love and to help us understand that all life has value?

Part Two: Transitions

Like the glowing embers that linger from a once flaming fire, I watched as my mother's vibrant life neared its end. It was in the dog days of the hot summer of 2011. We had had many tearful goodbyes to the mother, friend, sister, grandmother, and great-grandmother that she was. Her later years had been immensely challenging. Mom had a disease they call "Alzheimer's," and her journey served up a mixed bag of experiences for all of us who loved her. But now, I can see that her "disease" was, in fact, a catalyst for my own spiritual expansion. It brought to me an adventure of struggles and sorrow, but also epiphanies and enlightenment.

It was on a Saturday in mid-August when I stood beside her, knowing that my mother was within hours of taking her final breath. She'd long since stopped eating and was in the labored-breathing stage. I stood up and moved closer to her, looking up and down her body, head to foot. I tried to memorize every part of her, including the scars. My attention was drawn to her hands, which were disfigured from years of rheumatoid arthritis. I picked them up, held them, and remembered the times when they made sweet apple pies, held and rocked us, and wiped away our tears. Never had these hands stopped loving babies, although recently, the ones she loved were baby dolls that she believed to be real.

A wave of appreciation struck me as I thought about her body being the place where I began my earthly life. I knew any moment could be the last for seeing my mother physically alive. I combed her hair with my fingers, and my mind flooded with fond memories of her. I began to hum the song she always sang to rock my baby brother to sleep. My tears flowed down my face and fell onto her body. How ironic it was that she had first protected and cared for me, and now I was doing the same for her. The finality of her departure hit me. My tears increased. I found myself remembering the countless Saturdays Leslie and I had enjoyed with her, both before and after her dementia. My humming broke into singing out loud and I began to stroke her forehead and massage her arms. I glanced around the home, from the living room to the dining room, and I recalled many wonderful memories of holidays spent with my mom and my dad, who passed away some thirty years before. I was keenly aware that I was standing in our final moment together, in this place, and before morning came, my mother died.

In grieving the loss of my mother, I was surprised to find that I was actually grieving the loss of my two mothers: the earlier one and the later one, whom I had come to thoroughly enjoy. These moms had vastly different, yet loveable, personalities. I missed my "old mom" and I missed my "new mom." I had assumed that in accepting my "new mom," I had released my attachment to my "old mom." But that was not the case. Yes, my expansive spiritual perspective had helped me to accept this "new mom," but I had not actually released my attachment to my "old mom." My unexpected pain alerted me to this unfinished business and I fell into a many-layered grieving process.

With the time I'd previously spent attending to my mom, I reflected upon the many lessons she'd brought to me. I can now see that we stand to learn so much from individuals with Alzheimer's and other "disabilities." They can inspire us to express the sweet joys of our soul, to exude the calm of a peaceful inner life, and to bring happiness to the world around us. I saw connections between the families of loved ones with developmental disabilities and families of loved ones with Alzheimer's. It was becoming clear to me that the individuals with developmental disabilities, such as autism and Down syndrome, and with Alzheimer's "disease," were freer to be their authentic selves than the rest of us. Those who acquire these "disabilities" seem to cease their worry over what others are thinking, which allows a state of perpetual authenticity. They can dance more harmoniously to the soulful music of their inner beings than we normal folk. Furthermore, regardless of the happenings in their external world, they are determined to do whatever is necessary to remain tuned in to their radiant, joyful selves.

Now that's a teacher.

It may sound bizarre to some, but I highly recommend that anyone seeking spiritual expansion seek an occasion to observe these amazing people with Alzheimer's, autism, and Down syndrome. It is masterful work, and it can be watched and learned. Most of these teachers are able to release their resistance to the outer world by tuning into their more peaceful inner world. They are practicing and teaching us what the great spiritual teachers have been saying for centuries: that the "the kingdom of heaven is within." Society has trained us to behave in specified ways and thereby suppress our authentic inner selves. If we overcome such peer pressure and allow our true selves to shine, we can sow seeds of joy in our being, and our harvest will be boundless joy.

Those who have loved ones experiencing these "disabilities" or "diseases" have a big decision to make. They can place their loved one in a care giving home, never visit and try to forget about them. Or they can become martyrs and begrudgingly care for their family member. Or they can make peace with what is and begin to reap the gifts from this fertile and beautiful soul. I heartily recommend the third, life-enhancing choice.

After the initial shock of losing my old, familiar mother, I worked to accept my new mother. In time, I came to appreciate her new characteristics. And finally, I became completely at peace with my "new mom" and our new relationship, and I began to relish the lessons she was giving me. I can now say that this experience was a fulfilling

CHAPTER 3

Common Definitions of Autism Spectrum Disorder & Alzheimer's Disease

~ Nancy Reder RN & Fern Farinho

Autism is usually a lifelong neurological disorder that can affect an individual's ability to interact socially, to communicate and/or understand language, and typically includes restricted and repetitive interests and/or behaviors. It is important to know that every individual with autism is unique. While there are some characteristics that are common in autism, they vary widely in each individual.

Autism is classified as a developmental disability because of the way it impacts the pattern of a child's development. Diagnostic criteria states that certain symptoms must be apparent before the child is three years of age, in order to receive a diagnosis of autism (CDC, 2009).

The wide range of type and severity of symptoms in individuals with autism has led to the change of the sole use of the word "autism," to the term Autism Spectrum Disorder (ASD). ASD includes individuals who have severe, moderate, or mild symptoms. While some individuals may have severe behaviors and are non-verbal, others have a mild form known as Asperger's Syndrome.

ASD varies significantly in character and severity; it occurs in all ethnic and socioeconomic groups and affects every age group. Experts estimate that one out of 88 children under age eight will be diagnosed with ASD (Baio, 2012). Male children are four times more likely to have ASD than female children.

Although there is no cure for ASD, early intervention, therapies, and behavioral interventions are designed to promote substantial improvement. While interventions help individuals with ASD reach their full potential, these individuals typically continue to need services and supports throughout their lifetime. The proper supports allow many individuals to work successfully and live independently, or in a supported environment ("Autism fact sheet," 2012).

A nationwide study has found that intensive early intervention therapy is effective for improving cognition and language skills among very young children with autism and that it also normalizes their brain activity, decreases their symptoms, and improves their social skills, (Dawson, 2012).

Pervasive developmental disorder (PDD-NOS) is a general term that refers to a category of disorders in which autism is the best known. This also includes:

- **Asperger syndrome:** Form of autism with normal language development.
- **Rett syndrome:** Common among females where there is a dysfunction in the nervous system.
- **Childhood disintegrative disorder:** A rare condition where the disability occurs after the development of normal skills, and then loses them by age 10.

Characteristics of ASD

- Insistence on sameness: easily overwhelmed by minimal changes in routines, sensitive to environmental stressors, preference for rituals.
- Impairment in social interactions: difficulty understanding the "rules" of interaction, poor comprehension of jokes and metaphor, pedantic speaking style.
- Restricted range of social competence: preoccupation with singular topics, asking repetitive questions, obsessively collecting items.
- Inattention: poor organizational skills, easily distracted, focused on irrelevant stimuli, difficulty learning in group contexts.
- Poor motor coordination: slow clerical speed, clumsy gait, unsuccessful in games involving motor skills.
- Academic difficulties: restricted problem-solving skills, literal thinking, deficiencies with abstract reasoning.
- Emotional vulnerability: low self-esteem, easily overwhelmed, poor coping with stressors, self-critical.
  (Dr. Deborah Witt Turner's Power Point)

Savant Syndrome is a unique but phenomenal condition in which persons can have significant intellectual impairment, including Autism Spectrum Disorder but have an ability of genius. These gifted individuals, despite their often severely incapacitating disabilities in communication, social, and on occasions, intellectual development, often display extraordinary gifts or splinter skills in one or several domains.

Savant gift—or splinter skills—may be displayed in the following areas or domains: astounding memory, hyperlexia (e.g. the exceptional ability to read, spell, or write), art, music, mechanical or spatial skill, calendar calculation, mathematical calculation, sensory sensitivity, athletic performance, and computer ability. These skills may be amazing in comparison to the disability of autism.

As many as one in ten persons with Autism Spectrum Disorder have such impressive abilities to varying extents, although savant syndrome occurs in other developmental disabilities and in other types of central nervous system injuries or disease.

Around 10% of people with autism show special or even remarkable skills (Strahan, 2006).

In both of our professional careers, Ken and I have seen autistic and autistic/savant skills exhibited. It is an experience one never forgets. To view a perfectly scaled drawing of a brick house, hear perfectly replicated music played by untrained musicians, have the day of the week of your birth accurately identified within a few seconds from providing your birth date ... all leave you with a sense of awe and fascination. You want more for the sheer beauty of their skills. What wondrous gifts they give us! Our world would be less exciting and innovative without them—a true loss for humanity.

Definition of Alzheimer's Disease

Alzheimer's disease (AD) is a brain disorder that is similar to dementia. It is characterized by memory loss, severe behavioral changes and currently has no cure.

Most often, AD is diagnosed in people over 65 years of age, although the less prevalent early-onset Alzheimer's disease can occur much earlier. In 2006, there were 26.6 million suffers worldwide. Alzheimer's disease is predicted to affect 1 in 85 people globally by 2050 (Brookmeyer, Ziegler-Graham, Johnson & Arrighi, 2007).

AD knows no social, ethnic, or racial discrimination. We are all vulnerable to a greater or lesser degree.

Although Alzheimer's disease develops differently for every individual, there are many common symptoms (Alzheimer's Society, 2012). Early symptoms are often mistakenly thought to be age-related concerns, or manifestations of stress. In the early stages, the most common symptom is difficulty in remembering recent events. When AD is suspected, the diagnosis is usually confirmed with tests that evaluate behavior and thinking abilities, often followed by a brain scan if available.

As the disease advances, symptoms can include confusion, irritability and aggression, mood swings, trouble with language, and long-term memory loss.

Since the disease is different for each individual, predicting how it will affect the person is difficult. AD develops for an unknown and variable amount of time before becoming fully apparent, and it can progress undiagnosed for years. On the average, the life expectancy is approximately seven years. Fewer than three percent of individuals live more than fourteen years after diagnosis (Molsa, Marttila, & Rinne, 1986, p. 103-107).

The cause and progression of Alzheimer's are not well understood. Research indicates that the disease is associated with plaques and tangles in the brain (Tiraboshi, et al., 2004, p. 1984-9).

Current treatments only help with the symptoms of the disease. There are no available treatments that stop or reverse the progression of the disease. As of 2013, more than 1000 clinical trials have been or are being conducted to find ways to treat the disease, but it is unknown if any of the tested treatments will work (National Institute of Health, 2013).

Along with a healthy lifestyle of good nutrition and exercise, mental stimulation is suggested as ways to delay symptoms, but to date there is no conclusive evidence that supports an effect on the prevention or slowing of the progression of the disease.

In our gathering of journeys we have been amazed at the innovative and compassionate interventions that are being implemented on behalf of people with AD and dementia.

From music, to art, to theatre and appropriate social enhancements—all improve the quality of life and may also diminish the heart-breaking effects loved ones and caregivers experience during this difficult time.

Where are the gifts? Do we give our gift of loving the "new" person in a different way, but no less? How do our lives change from the challenge, and do we have an opportunity for growth in our personal lives? More questions than answers, certainly, but therein lies the journey.

Does the person with Alzheimer's and/or dementia give love and acceptance through the journey in a new way? The gifts they give us may be difficult to discern, and questionable, but then don't we all give and receive gifts differently?

It appears to be a circle of giving and accepting, broken only by one's end of life.

Thank you, on behalf of those with Alzheimer's, to all those who provide quality of life opportunities, and experience the emotional, financial, and spiritual challenges you are greeted with.

The Alzheimer's Challenge

With all my respect I pay tribute to Ken's mother, Fern, a loving and amazing lady, a loving mother and great friend known by many, famous for her strong and sensitive personality.

But it is refreshing to be remembered by the ones who knew her and loved her and were loved by her.

Like many people, Fern's life was taken away by the condition called Alzheimer's disease. Alzheimer's is the most common form of dementia among older people. Dementia is as brain disorder that seriously affects a person's ability to carry out daily activities.

Alzheimer's begins slowly. It first involves parts of the brain that control thought, memory, and language. People with Alzheimer's may have trouble remembering things that happened recently or names of people they know.

A related problem, mild cognition impairment (MCI), causes more memory problems than normal for people of the same age. Many, but not all, people with MCI will develop Alzheimer's.

In Alzheimer's, over time, symptoms get worse. People may not recognize family members or have trouble speaking, reading, or writing. They may forget how to brush their teeth or comb their hair. Later on, they may become anxious or aggressive or wander away from home. Eventually, they need total care, which can cause great emotional and financial stress for the family members who must care for them.

Alzheimer's usually begins after age 60, and the risk increases with age. Your risk is also higher if a family member has had the disease. No treatment can stop the disease. However, some drugs may help keep symptoms from getting worse for a limited time.

When you learn that someone that you know has Alzheimer's, you may wonder when and how to tell your family and friends. You may be worried about how others will react to or treat the person. My advice is to realize that family and friends often sense that something is wrong before they are told. Alzheimer's disease is hard to keep a secret—there is no single right way to tell others about Alzheimer's. When it seems right, be honest with family, friends and others. Use this chance to educate them about Alzheimer's. Tell friends and family about Alzheimer's disease and its effects. Share articles, websites, and other information about the disease, and tell them what they can do to help. Let them know when you need breaks from caregiving.

When a family member has Alzheimer's, it affects everyone in the family, including children and grandchildren. It is important to talk to everyone affected about what is happening. Here are some tips to help family and friends to understand how to interact with the person with Alzheimer's:

- Help the family and friends realize what the person can still do and how much he or she can understand.

- Give visitors suggestions about how to start talking with the person. For example, tell them to make eye contact and say, "Hello Lucy. I'm Mary. We used to work together."

I learned a lot based on my personal experience with a first cousin and many years of working and teaching in healthcare.

Prayer for the Loss of a Loved One

Dear God,

Experiencing the loss of a loved one is so shattering.

It is so difficult to greet each day when my loss has left me empty and numb.

Help me fill that void with the focus of the wonderful memories we shared.

Allow me to feel the comfort and gentle encouragement of your angels whispering that my loved one is safe and happy with
Please nourish me with your love and give me the strength and will to carry on.

Amen

By: Fern Farinho
Medical Instructor/Program Developer/Placement Coordinator, National Academy of Health and Business

CHAPTER 4

Individual Perspectives on Autism

Life with Autism - Emerging Through the Haze
Paul Isaacs

My name is Paul Isaacs, I'm 27 years old and I have a diagnosis of High Functioning Autism in 2010 and Scotopic Sensitivity Syndrome in 2012. I would like to contribute to *The Gifts of Autism and Alzheimer's: Stories of Unconditional Love and Self-Determination* the gifts and the unique perceptions I have on the world around me.

During my younger years it was clear I was different from a typical child. I was a late walker and it took me 18 months to start before that I used to use my right arm to pull myself along the sitting room floor. I was a late speaker; I didn't gain functional speech until 7 or 8 years old and didn't gain functional receptive speech until I was 10 or 11 years old.

As a child I would have had a diagnosis of *Classic Autism*, as I lived (and continue to live) in a sensory-based world where all objects are fragmented and meaning of my surrounding is gained through touching, sniffing, tapping, rubbing, licking, mouthing and gazing at objects for a long periods of time. I enjoyed activities which involved kinaesthetic play, such as painting

My Father and I at a family holiday in 1989. I had *classic autism*. © Isaacs Family

primary colours with my hands, feeling surfaces with my bare feet, skimming at water—one of my first intense interests was water. I had a deep unconditional bond with this formless, flowing mass. I consider it my first friend and I had this love for water for many years.

I also liked to mold play dough in my hands over and over again. This made me feel happy and at ease with the world. I had a single focus which was not with people but with objects, however, I trusted people whom understood me from an early age. I thank my parents, who are also on the spectrum, for always being there for me and believing in me.

Between 2002 and 2008, I had many unsuccessful jobs, but my talents were yet to flourish. In late 2009, after seeing an advertisement in a local Autism base about young people talking about their lives on the spectrum, I decided to pursue this prospect. In January 2010 I presented my first speech for Autism Oxford. It's the first time in my life that I had found my niche. I have a talent which gives me great happiness and pleasure. I enjoy presenting speeches for the sole reason of improving the lives of people on the autism spectrum. That is my goal and I now consider it a life's goal!

At my first speaking event in 2010
© Isaacs, Erangey, Autism Oxford

I have presented speeches for Autism Oxford and other Autism-based charities and organizations. I have also presented training and consultancy covering many topics such as challenging behaviors, sensory issues, relationships and friendships, mental health, employment, life story with autism, autism and agnosia (using *Donna Williams' Fruit Salad Model* © 1995), question and answer sessions and so forth.

Why did this happen? Because people had belief, acceptance, empathy and commitment. They could see that I had talent before I even knew it myself. That's what I want to give to people on the spectrum: the right to happy, content and live a life which is free from barriers, where they're understood for their autism and the qualities they can bring.

I have also presented online webinar presentations with Craig Evans of *Autism Hangout* and Kathleen Tehrani of *Autism Brainstorm*. I thank them for their time and commitment to positive Autism awareness.

My Books: *Living Through The Haze*
I found my talent for words, and I have published an autobiography entitled *Living through the Haze: Life on the Autistic Spectrum*. I am also a speaker at events. This has given me a purpose in life. And I believe everyone has a purpose, including people on the spectrum!

I am very grateful to all the people, such as my parents, for loving me for who I am. Donna Williams for her wisdom and knowledge, and all her help during the early years of understanding my own Autism. She has helped so many people on the spectrum. Kathy Erangey, Manager and Director of Autism Oxford, saw my potential in 2009. She has a helped me so much over the years, paving the way for Autism services along with all the Autism Oxford training team.

Living through the Haze: Life on the Autistic Spectrum is about my life on the spectrum from non-verbal child to adult.

In 2012 I was diagnosed with Scotopic Sensitivity Syndrome by a James Billett, who specialises in the field of tinted lenses for people with learning difficulties, developmental disabilities and other conditions. Within the diagnosis many agnosia were recognised:

• Simultagnosia (Object Blindness)
• Semantic Agnosia (Meaning Blindness)
• Prosopagnosia (Face Blindness)
• Visual Verbal Agnosia (Comprehension Blindness)

Also learning difficulties were recognised also:
• Dyslexia
• Dyscalculia

Life Through A Kaleidoscope
James Billett and I went on to collaborate on my 2nd published book entitled *Life Through A Kaleidoscope*. This book gives an in depth personal and professional take on visual sensory issues for a person on the Autistic Spectrum. I was very pleased to have

met James and will be forever grateful for his help in recognizing my visual sensory issues.

A Pocket Size Practical Guide for Parents, Professionals and People on The Autistic Spectrum

My third book was initiated through meeting with Prof. Tony Attwood in 2012 at an Autism Oxford Event. I asked him if he could look at a manuscript and would he be interested in writing a foreword for it. I was amazed that later that year when he did.

This book is an easy-to-read, practical guide for people in the world of Autism, including people on the spectrum themselves. It covers many topics, from public transport, shopping in stores, to personal hygiene, giving hints and tips on each chapter in practical format. I wanted to give something back to help others on the spectrum.

Overall, the one thing in life I have learned is the importance of being happy with yourself and the importance of helping others and giving something back to society in whatever you can. I leave you with this passage:

"Do not fear people with Autism, embrace them, Do not spite people with Autism unite them, Do not deny people with Autism accept them for then their abilities will shine."

Links
Autism Oxford www.autismoxford.com
Chipmunka Book Publishers chipmunkapublishing.co.uk
National Autistic Society UKwww.autism.org.uk
Autism Hangout www.autismhangout.com
Autism Brainstorm www.autismbrainstorm.org

Who Am I? - Getting to Know Me
John Denges

There are many challenges in the world. Climbing Mt. Everest; the New York Times Sunday crossword puzzle; trying to understand why hot dogs come in packs of ten and hot dog buns in packs of twelve. Well, there's another: getting to know me. Now I'll admit that it's not on the same level as Everest and crosswords, but since I don't open up easily to people, getting to know the kind of person I am isn't very easy. So, while I have this chance (along with the fact that I'm getting graded on this), I might as well present parts of who I am to you to read.

A miswired computer

One of the major things about me is that I have Asperger Syndrome, which is a high-functioning form of Autism. It's a neuro-biological disorder that affects how the brain operates. To put it simply, the Aeperger's brain is like a computer with its wiring done a little outside what is considered standard. Some parts of the brain can operate at a level that is above average in society, but other parts do not develop as well as the average person's.

One of the most common areas that doesn't fully develop is social interaction. The average person has a kind of instinct that develops on its own that allows them to interact with other people verbally and non-verbally. A person with Asperger's may still be able to communicate verbally, but will not understand what is taboo in a conversation. Non-verbal communication skills tend to be even worse. The subtle facial expressions and other physical signs that may be picked up easily by the average person will likely go undetected by someone with Asperger's.

Also, because of this "miswiring" one's way of thinking can be different from the average person's. Some have described it as thinking in pictures; I prefer to say that my logic comes from a different perspective.

When I found out

I would go so far as to say that the day I was diagnosed with this condition was one of the best days of my life. Before this discovery, life for me was difficult to say the least. I possessed very few friends; never had a long relationship with a significant other, and finding my place in the workforce was miserable for me. I knew something about me was off, but I had no idea what.

Try to imagine driving around and something is telling you that there is a problem with your car, but no one can find anything wrong. You know in your gut that there is a problem, but until it can be found, it just eats away at you. It becomes such a relief when the problem is finally discovered and addressed. That was what it was like for me. I felt that there was something wrong about me, but not knowing what it was made me crazy. How could I fix what was wrong when I couldn't figure out what it was?

That's why it was such a relief when the diagnosis of Asperger's was made. Before that, I never heard of the condition, but as I read more and more about it, it seemed to describe me and my problems perfectly, from being bullied as a kid to being obsessed on certain things instead of a general interest in a lot of stuff. Not only did I now know what was wrong with me, I could now figure out how to go about "fixing" it. It was a relief to my dad as well. All these years he wondered what he did wrong or what he could've done differently in raising me. Now he knows that he's not to blame in any way for all the negative ways I turned out.

Since my diagnosis, I've come a long way with the treatment I received. I am more open and talkative than I ever was growing up. My confidence has gone up as well. I still have problems in some areas, but it is as they say, "Rome wasn't built in a day."

That's what I like

Like everyone else, I do have my likes and dislikes (I just need to remember not to become obsessed with them.) I enjoy almost all kinds of music (except opera.) My IPod has over 2,500 songs stored in it, from country to classic rock, heavy metal to jazz, hip-hop to pop, and Andrew Lloyd Weber to Jimmy Buffett. What's more, I can jump around genres at the drop of a hat. One minute I could be listening to Metallica, and then I could be switching to Toby Keith.

Video games are a good escape for me. They tend to stimulate both my imagination and problem-solving abilities. They allow me to imagine myself in the role of the hero by controlling him, unlike what you might experience in a movie, and find solutions to problems in my own way instead of just watching the hero do it himself.

Normally, I consider myself a t-shirt and jeans kind of guy and don't care about labels (especially since most of them are ridiculously priced beyond what I can afford). But I'll admit to a couple of labels I tend to stick to. I've worn Wrangler jeans for the longest time because they've been the most durable and comfortable brand I've worn. That and they're a big sponsor to my favorite race car drivers Dale Earnhardt Jr. and his dad, the late Dale Earnhardt Sr.

Nike is the other label I'll admit to because they've made excellent products. They originally made just shoes, which were made for any kind of foot, but soon branched out into other things. Their sunglasses are the most comfortable I've ever worn and their apparel is made to keep you comfortable in any condition. They also sponsor many of my favorite athletes, from basketball's Lebron James to Maria Sharapova to Sarah Reinertsen.

What motivates me?

Sarah Reinertsen is a triathlete who is also an amputee. When Sarah was a child, well before the age of ten, she had to have her left leg amputated and learn how to walk with a prosthetic leg. While growing up, Sarah was determined not to let her disability prevent her from playing sports, so she worked hard and became a track star at her school. Later, she took the next step and began competing in triathlons. In 2004, she made her first attempt in completing the Ironman Triathlon in Hawaii. Even though she failed to complete it that year, she didn't give up. After a year of training and some improvements in her bike equipment, in 2005 she successfully completed the Ironman. That's inspirational and a reminder for me that I can prevent my disability from holding me backs.

Another motivational tool I use involves another of my likes—cars. When I started owning a car, I grew to appreciate the intangibles of it, like what the car says about me. For most of this past decade, I've been into the sport-compact culture, where you take a four-cylinder import and modify it with both performance and cosmetic parts and accessories. However, I soon realized how expensive a lot of these parts were. I decided to not do anything to my car's engine so I wouldn't hurt the resale value when it's time to trade it in. In the last year or so, I've gotten caught up in the return of the American muscle car and have fallen in love with the new Camaro. I do want to own one—I know that in my current situation that would not be possible. That's why I use it as a motivational tool. I remind myself that if I want to be able to afford one, I have got to work hard to get past my disabilities and become a successful member of the workforce. Even if that is not enough for me to get the Camaro, I'll know that it helped get me to a better state of being.

Well, that's me in a nutshell. I hope that you, the reader, picked up on some things about me and learned to understand me a little better.

A Journey of Answers - Excerpts from *More than a Shadow*
Nancy Getty
In 1959, I was born the fourth of six children in a Canadian Armed Forces family. The life of a military family generally would have the family posting to different bases, but after I was born my family stayed on the same base until my father's retirement fifteen years later.

As a child, I learned quickly to follow not only the family rules but also the rules set out by the military base. Many areas of the base were considered out of bounds as well, and curfews were strictly enforced.

The strict upbringing and regulated rules worked well for me since I appreciated the sameness of the "rules." Sameness was very difficult to achieve socially. Families and classmates were known to me for a short timeframe before they were posted away, so for the first fifteen years of my life, it was very difficult to attempt to form any balance in relationships. In school, I also struggled with many classroom issues and found it difficult to express my answers verbally or to perform well in group settings. Throughout my junior years of school, my report cards, commonly used words such as "lazy," "stupid," "unfocused," "daydreamer," "puts very little effort into her work" and "is disruptive." I personally liked the word "precocious" since it had a regal sound to it, although as a child I did not realize that it was not a good label to be associated with. I was to spend much of my school days sitting in the principal's office where many times I would receive the strap for being disruptive and disobedient. I was never really sure what I had done, since no one took the time to explain what I was being punished for or what I should change. I grew to expect and accept the punishment and no longer looked to question the reasons. Bullying escalated over those junior years since the other children quickly learned that I was an easy target and the teachers had already flagged me as the problem. I now believe that these past experiences are what rooted the internal strength and unbreakable spirit that I have carried throughout my life.

In 1990, I gave birth to twins, a girl and a boy, and within one month of their birth, I became a single mother of my children. How was I to raise, guide and protect them? The answer came when I approached a government agency to apply for financial aide. They suggested that I place my children in foster care since my apparent differences would make it difficult for me to raise them. "What apparent differences? No one is going to take my family from me, I will find a way!" This was my only response as I rose and left the office. I could never have foreseen the future of where this new

Nancy Getty and her family.

journey in my life was to lead but I was determined to be a good parent. Little did I know that this would become a journey of trials, tribulations, struggle, and most of all, answers.

I found three jobs at different horse farms where I would clean the stalls and barn, feed the animals and do turnouts six days a week. Each morning, I would rise at 5a.m., feed my children, get them dressed, pack the car and head out to the first farm. I would set up the playpen in an empty stall where the kids were both safe and I could see them. I would stop to play with them, feed and change them and tend to their needs. The first barn had over 30 horses so the bulk of our day was spent there. But as soon as I was done, we were packed and heading to the second barn which had 15 horses and then onto the last barn where there were 4 horses. We would arrive home at approximately 6 p.m. After supper and bath time, it was "our time" in which we enjoyed each other and appreciated every moment together.

This was to be our routine for the next three years until it became difficult to tend to my children's growing needs and continue to do this type of work. I began a new seasonal job with a lawn care company and hired an "at home" sitter. Since this worked well for all of us, I then took a seasonal factory job during the winter months. I managed, but financial difficulties made life a teetering game in paying bills, feeding and caring for two children, and with the added strain of physical labor, I was exhausted. I worked through the pain and minor injuries with a looming fear that if I failed, an agency may try to take my children from me due to the differences "they" felt were apparent. I could not fail since my children were my world, my focus.

At the age of eight my son was diagnosed with Asperger Syndrome. During the testing process of the diagnosis, it was suggested that they also suspected that, if formally tested, I would receive the same diagnosis. First of all, I had no idea what Asperger Syndrome was and secondly, I was more interested in understanding my son's needs than my own, so I showed little interest in being tested. Thus began my research into seeking answers to assist my child who was struggling in many aspects of his life. Within society, differences are shunned and feared due to the lack of knowledge and understanding. But the more I read about this mysterious disorder, the more I discovered and was comforted by the similarities that also described my own perceptions and traits: Asperger Syndrome, a neurological disorder on the Autism Spectrum. My research into discovering the challenges my son was encountering was actually opening a door to understanding my own challenges. I became angry, saddened and elated in a blend of overwhelming emotions. As I furthered my research and began to understand ASD, my past began to make sense. Why didn't anyone else know or notice? Why did I have to endure such misunderstanding and hardships? Why? How can I make a difference for my son so he does not have to follow in my footsteps? So many questions but I knew I was definitely capable of discovering the answers and that my children's future depended on it.

Despite my growing self awareness and my son's diagnosis, the three of us enjoyed everything we had to offer to each other; we relished life. As time passed, I witnessed the growth of the beautiful spirit within my children as individuals. Their laughter filled the air and their unique personalities began to shine through bringing a gift of purity, honesty and sensitivity. As a person that had been chastised and shunned in my youth, I developed strategies to assist them so they would not struggle in the same areas. Social expectations such as eye contact were very important to possess, so I would always face them towards each other and we played mirror games where we made strange faces and had to guess what the emotion the person was portraying. Manners were important, since I knew that even if they were unsure of a social situation, by being polite, the outcome tends to be more positive.

I began their schooling early at home using a hands-on approach with visual aides such as documentary films. I promoted reading, explaining to them that there is a power in words and understanding the words is the root to creating self understanding and an inner strength. Our home was a happy and safe place where passions were fed and creativity was cherished. My son showed early art skills and with a fascination for aircraft, he slowly began to hone his artistic talents as well as his knowledge base for strategies and the history of armed conflict. His grandfather provided the exciting stories from his days in the military and my son's drawings of airplanes and fact based WW2 air battles developed into precise history lessons. His sister was very meticulous and could see a finished craft project from a pile of paper or material scraps and thus was born her first interest as a juvenile clothing designer. Since her other passion and comfort was being within the company of animals, our dogs, cats and rabbits would become the fashion models for her unique creations. One of the rules I had decided to follow as a parent was to guide but never push my children. To allow their individual selves to blossom from the roots I helped them plant, and to stand beside them, nurture and support their natural growth. They grew to stand strong against the wind, the rain, and the storms.

At the age of 43, I received a formal diagnosis of Asperger Syndrome. With that diagnosis, I walked through the open door to understanding Autism Spectrum Disorders and by doing so, I hoped that my family may then have opportunity to succeed within society. I was going to learn, continue to assist my children and then I would teach others so that other children would be understood and not chastised for their differences. But how was I to accomplish such a grand undertaking? I now had an extended purpose but I needed a plan.

In 2008, I gave my first presentation to a small group of childcare workers. By now, my daughter had also received a diagnosis of Asperger Syndrome (which came as no surprise to her brother and I) and with this, my determination only grew stronger. As I write this, I have presented across Canada to large audiences and been part of radio and television interviews as I bring non-clinical awareness and understanding of the challenges and strengths of ASD. With creation of my website, www.aspergerrus.com, the response to further awareness of ASD has been surreal. This has been the most exhausting and fearful quest that I have ever attempted, aside from raising two caring, kind and honest children, of whom I am very proud. I have forced myself to face my own fears, calm my anxieties and find the courage and understanding to become the tool that translates between the typical world and the autistic world. I could not have done all this without the care and support of the friends currently in my life.

The message I bring begins with my mantra: "Differences are meant to be discovered and understood. Once understood, they are no longer just differences." I came to realize, this was not a journey I could take alone. I needed to build a choir. I was one voice but if others could understand and take their knowledge forward, we could sing louder together. Collectively, we could be heard!

What is autism....a difference! What is typical...a difference! What is normal?

We live in the most confusing environment. Everything around us—at home, in the media, schools, everywhere you look and listen—we are told to follow our passion. "Follow what is inside of you; what brings you comfort, let that be your guide." If you're a writer, then you should write about what you know, what you enjoy, what you are passionate about. If you are a painter, paint beyond what is obvious, paint what you see. Musician, actor, teacher, community worker, service worker, tradesman, executive! Find the thing you are good at, study, practice and push forward. These are the messages that we receive, yet they are mixed with the expectations of society. To learn a certain way, to not obsess in one area, to do it the way it has been done for many, many years. "Don't rock the boat!"

Then there are the social expectations, be polite, don't argue, respect others, walk away, do as you are told, do not question authority, be seen and not heard, obey! Then you are told, think for yourself, use your own judgment, try it on your own, stand up for yourself, question what you believe to be wrong, speak up, and make a difference! I am so confused!

When? How? Where? Under which circumstances do the conflicting rules apply? Who do you ask when you already feel misunderstood? How do you ask? Is it your own perception that is incorrect or is there a possibility that you may have the right answer but have never felt that you could be the one to make a difference?

I really wish I had the answers to all of these questions. I wish I knew why society does not make it easier to function. When you already have differences that have you standing apart from others, the confusion escalates. So what do you do?

My vote is, follow the thing that you obsess over, are passionate about and find a way to use it to improve your life and the lives of others. Follow your passion! There is nothing wrong with "flipping burgers" if that is what you are comfortable with, but go one more step and take a food handler's course. Learn as many aspects of the company you work for, as you can. Remember politeness but do not be afraid to be strong if anyone is belittling you. Disagree if you have the knowledge in the area of the debate but do so with respect for the other person's opinions and ideas. Yes, use your own judgment but also use the knowledge of others. Try to follow the rules that are set out to guide you and keep you safe. Voice your ideas but be willing to try it "The other way." There are many people that are ruled by the paycheck, but there are just as many that have followed their passion and remain passionate. I am living proof that individuals on the spectrum can excel, function very well and add to society when they follow the area of expertise that is personal to them.

For those that are guiding or supporting an individual on the spectrum, assist with effective communication, develop the strategies and find the tools that will help the ASD individual combat their sensory sensitivities. By removing these roadblocks the individual will be able to reach their full potential. Never underestimate the hard work and effort that an individual on the spectrum puts forth every moment of every day. The anxiety and sensory experiences are an exhausting struggle that is unique to each person, yet they push through at a level that is vast in strength and perseverance. Supporting the family of an ASD individual is an important aspect of autism, since autism affects the entire family as a unit. The connections we make throughout our lives are pieces of a puzzle that creates the picture of who we are. If we work together we can all enjoy the process of building and adding to the masterpiece of the human spirit.

It does not have to be "US" and "THEM." Everyone is trying, some harder than others, to change the way society teaches, learns, and makes a difference to assist others. Altruism is a powerful word, a powerful concept! But to step outside your comfort zone and to actually live a life of extending forward the acts of altruism within society takes courage. Learn and be accepting of the diversities within society. Instead of just making the change, be the change. The differences we discover within society do not have to remain a mystery. Those who take a positive approach and deny conformity are our teachers. Learn from them, do not stigmatize that which may teach you your greatest lesson.

I never believed that I had worth. I always knew I had determination and an unbridled spirit, but worth? Never! Meeting the standards and expectations set out by society crushed my confidence until I became but a shadow. A shadow that wore masks to function at a time when lack of supports, misunderstanding of differences, and swift punishment for stepping outside the norm pushed me from the light that shone deep inside of me. We all wear masks but when the masks are worn out of fear, to avoid inevitable failure and punishment, they are masks of a captive person.

I have found my purpose and, with knowledge, understanding, determination, support and courage, I have found my worth through an unselfish regard for and to the devotion and welfare of others. Altruism! Now that I know better, I choose to do better. And for as many times as I have fallen there is the same number of times that I have stood up again. Failure is inevitable! That is how we learn and become stronger and more appreciative of success. I will succeed to make a positive difference. As one voice, I will stand in the light and sing loud from the song in my heart.

I am ... More than a shadow.

Nancy Getty
A.S.P.I.E.S.
www.aspergerrus.com

If there is anything that we wish to change in the child, we should first examine it and see whether it is not something that could better be changed in ourselves.
Carl Jung

CHAPTER 5

The Gifts of Art and Music

Music is truly the universal language. Music has enlightened, inspired, motivated, empowered, and entertained many cultures and civilizations throughout human existence. Freedom, nature, and music empower me. My favorite time is Spring with Mother Nature—the music of the birds, the vibrating pecking of the woodpeckers, the croaking of the frogs, the chirping of the crickets, the reverberations of resounding thunder, and the soothing rhythm of the gentle stream or the roar of the ocean waves. Nature, and therefore art, is a creative expression, reflection, and out-picturing of Father-Mother God!

You can see the metaphor of nature as art manifested in the face of detailed, decorated, colorful flowers, or the arms and legs of a majestic oak tree. (During my mom's Alzheimer's, she called tree trunks "legs.") Very awesome are the landscape scenes of magnificent mountains and the spectacular beauty and peacefulness of the oceans blue. Nature entertains and inspires us with its own theater by giving us chills when we gaze in awe and wonderment while observing the soaring of an eagle or a sunrise or sunset, as we are serenaded by the cacophony of sea birds and ocean waves in their joyful symphony. Humans and animals are offspring of this divine, all-powerful, extremely intelligent, loving and creative God.

We have been given the gifts of love and emotion. Just feel your emotions in awe as you watch a pet or your child being born. Music and art are also God's gift through human imagination and the ability to express, experience, and enjoy the talents of artists and musicians. People with autism and Alzheimer's express, experience, and enjoy naturally when they can no longer express themselves in the form of traditional communication. Many with autism are uninhibited, and people with Alzheimer's no longer are concerned with what other people think of them, so it is much easier for them to just enjoy the creativity of art, music, and theater.

Although these people at times may feel all alone in the Universe, I am beginning to believe that a part of them is inner-directed—and even though they may seem to be "staring out into space," they are feeling and seeing who they really are.

Music and art are natural therapy, for they can relax, sooth, revitalize, invigorate, inspire, and empower anyone who tunes in. Music has probably been my most effective tool for either establishing a harmonious environment that prevents behavioral issues or redirecting those who may be having a behavioral outburst.

I am currently working with a young woman who has a history of getting angry and hitting others. After I realized her natural gift was that of singing, all I have to do when she becomes agitated is ask her to share her beautiful voice. Her rage, anger and aggression disappear!

My favorite book on Alzheimer's, *I'm Still Here* by John Zeisel, Ph.D., talks about the wonder-filled program that he and his colleague Sean Caulfield founded called Artists for Alzheimer's (ARTZ). This program was designed for persons with Alzheimer's and their partners to take active participation in art and music opportunities throughout their own communities and was founded on the belief that access to creative expression is essential to our human experiences. The partnership includes artists, musicians, or just "regular folks" who volunteer to share their talents, either by helping others with their creative endeavors or by taking them to art museums or concerts.

The ARTZ website describes the program as one that links artists and cultural institutions to people living with dementia and their care partners. Influenced by science and sociology, ARTZ uses artistic experiences as keys to unlock creativity, create new memories, strengthen and develop relationships, and enrich lives in fundamental ways. ARTZ recognizes the wholeness that is inherent in each person regardless of a diagnosis and celebrates each person's capacity to participate in the journey of life.

In *I'm Still Here*, Dr. Zeisel provides illustrations of how art and music are naturally hardwired in the brain. Many abilities are lost throughout the various stages of deterioration; however the love and appreciation of art and music continues for some, even into death.

At the end of my mother's life, she could not swallow her food, her breathing had slowed, and she gradually lost her sense of consciousness. While propped up outside in her wheelchair just two days before her transition, although she spoke only a few sentences, in her own new language, she shared her heartfelt description of how beautiful the clouds and the tress were, and she tried to express her life-long appreciation of the natural music of her beloved birds. Music is hardwired in our brains and every fiber of our being as it connects us with our current culture, community, friends, and family with visceral memories.

During Glen Campbell's good-bye tour, my partner Leslie and I had the wonderful opportunity to see him in concert. His Alzheimer's was evident as he repeatedly would say he was having difficulty hearing himself and was expressing himself in a way that made no logical sense to the audience; nevertheless, when he picked up his guitar or banjo and began to play, it was if nothing was wrong. His voice and his music remained intact—his beautiful classics were hardwired into his brain!

I believe that the gifts of music and art can be the catalysts that bring those with autism and Alzheimer's closer to their loved ones, as well as sooth and ground all involved. It can also remind the friends and family members of those with Alzheimer's to remember and savor the time they have left and all the fond cherished memories that will carry us after their passing.

It has been my experience that many people with autism and Alzheimer's express themselves much better through art than through speech. I will never forget early in my career, a direct care worker approached me and said of a resident, "I see why he is diagnosed as ARTISTIC because he can draw better than anyone I have ever seen!" In his initial training, the care worker misunderstood and thought the instructor referred to the resident's artistic ability rather than his autistic diagnosis! But in a way, he was right!

Music anchors us to our past and to that of previous generations. How many of you can remember vividly where you were and what you were doing when you hear a certain song? Smells and nature are likewise hardwired and anchored to memories of our past. As Dr. Zeisel says:

> Art touches and engages the brain in a more profound way than other activities. Music, painting, sculpture, comedy, drama, poetry, and the other arts link together separate brain locations in which memories and skills lie. The brain systems affected in this way are therefore called "distributed." Music, for example, touches parts of the brain that link what we sense, know, and feel. As the brain is affected in Alzheimer's disease and particular locations and abilities are damaged, the fact that art touches so many areas of the brain masks single-locations deficits.
>
> The more someone is in touch with his or her feelings, the more he or she can appreciate art. The same is true for creating art. Artists who think too much edit their works mentally before they can express them. Because people living with Alzheimer's tend to express what they think and feel at the moment, they are natural artists and natural audiences for artistic expression.[1]

---

1   Zeisel, John, *I'm Still Here: A New Philosophy of Alzheimer's Care*, (New York, NY: Penguin Group, 2010), p. 81.

Does Everyone Have A Gift? Everyone has a gift!
What is your gift? What is their gift?
The greatest gifts are not materialistic, but the ones that each and every individual possesses and shares with others. Every human being is born with a gift. We may not always choose or be able to recognize these gifts for what they are, but they exist despite age, race, sex, disability, and other factors.

Anthony Robbins said: "Every problem is a gift—without problems we would not grow."

As the diagnostic rates for Autism Spectrum Disorders and Alzheimer's continue to soar, it is not surprising to hear about all the "problems" and concerns associated with these two diagnoses. Undeniably, there are similarities between Autism and Alzheimer's. Both of these diagnoses are associated with an array of physical, mental and emotional symptomology and characteristics that significantly affect not only the diagnosed individual, but also the individual's support system and loved ones.

Unfortunately, we rarely hear about the gifts or the unique abilities and skills that these individuals have been born with. These intrinsic gifts can in return evoke additional rewards, such as patience, understanding, and compassion from others. In all relationships, a reciprocal gift exchange occurs and has profound effect on all involved. By only focusing on the *problems*, many tend to overlook the gifts that each and every individual, even with a diagnosis, bestows.

Might a disability or disorder be accompanied by a gift? When it comes to individuals who have been diagnosed with an Autism Spectrum Disorder or Alzheimer's, it requires taking a closer look to gain some perspective. It's only at this point in time when one can begin to recognize the many gifts and experience the amazing joy that they bring to those around them. Any type of a diagnosis affects not only the individual but also those who care for him or her. Many who advocate for individuals diagnosed with Autism and Alzheimer's are empathetic, courageous, persistent, patient, and generous. Many advocate, whereas others adopt a devotion and determination to not allow the diagnosis and/or disabilities to inhibit their lives or diminish their self-worth. Are these qualities acquired by caregivers seen as problems or gifts that resulted from the diagnosis?

For those who have spent any amount of time in the company of individuals diagnosed with Alzheimer's or Autism, the similarities between the two conditions show striking parallels. While it is possible to identify many similarities with respect to the behaviors, symptomology, and characteristics, three specific areas which hold high rank in both diagnoses include:

Communication

Struggles with communication are often experienced by individuals diagnosed with Autism and Alzheimer's. These struggles can often leave others guessing as to what is trying to be expressed. The ability to express ideas and feelings, to find commonality, to communicate needs (whether verbally or non-verbally) and to indicate an understanding of others is a foundation for human relationships. Goal areas under the communication domain may include increasing receptive and expressive language, increasing emotional expression, and making known one's wants and needs.

Social Behaviors

Individuals diagnosed with both Autism and Alzheimer's often have difficulties differentiating between appropriate and inappropriate social behaviors. Certain individuals may be able to recognize socially inappropriate behavior, but have difficulty using spoken language to explain why the behaviors are unacceptable. It may be suggested that this decreased use of language may also make generalization of knowledge more difficult with respect to appropriate responses. Goals under the social behavior domain for individuals diagnosed with Autism and Alzheimer's may include increasing the likelihood for positive social interactions, decreasing inappropriate behaviors (verbal and/or physical aggression), and improving awareness of social roles and responsibilities.

Emotional and Behavioral Self-Regulation

Risk-taking and self-injurious behaviors are frequently associated with a diagnosis of Autism and/or Alzheimer's. Individuals who engage in self-injurious behaviors may directly inflict harm upon themselves. Some common self-injurious behaviors include biting, hair pulling, picking scabs and/or interfering with wound healing. Refusal and tantrums are also examples of poor self-regulation in escalated states. Emotional and behavioral self-regulation are skills which are imperative for one to acquire so as to maintain the safety and welfare of all individuals.

Despite the symptomology associated with Autism and Alzheimer's, engagement in the arts can enhance one's quality of life and functioning. This engagement, whether passive or active, can increase the recognition, identification, and thus the appreciation of gifts.

In the words of Michael Greene, President and CEO of NARAS - 1997 Grammy Awards:

When we look at the body of evidence that the arts contribute to our society, it's absolutely astounding. Music therapists are breaking down the walls of silence and affliction of Autism, Alzheimer's and Parkinson's disease.

Music Therapy is an established health profession in which music is used within a therapeutic relationship to address physical, emotional, cognitive, and social needs of individuals. Through musical involvement in the therapeutic context, clients' abilities are strengthened and transferred to other areas of their lives. Music therapy also provides avenues for communication that can be helpful to those who find it difficult to express themselves in words. Research in music therapy supports its effectiveness in many areas such as overall physical rehabilitation and facilitating movement, increasing an individual's motivation to become engaged in treatment, providing emotional support for clients and their families, and providing an outlet for expression of feelings. (AMTA)

According to the American Music Therapy Association, music therapy enhances one's quality of life, involving relationships between a qualified music therapist and individual; between one individual and another; between the individual and his/her family; and between the music and the participants. These relationships are structured and adapted through the elements of music to create a positive environment and set the occasion for successful growth.

In a famous YouTube video, Henry, an elderly man with dementia, is transformed by the power of music. Within only a few minutes of music from his youth, Henry seems to be miraculously brought out of his stupor. He gushes about his favorite jazz singer, sings a few verses in a rich baritone and waxes poetic about how music makes him feel.

In 2010, the researchers discovered that individuals diagnosed with Alzheimer's had a much easier time recalling song lyrics after words had been sung to them than they could after the words had been spoken. "It suggested that music might enhance new memory formation in patients," said Nicholas Simmons-Stern, also at Boston University and lead author of the study.

Similarly, individuals diagnosed with an Autism Spectrum Disorder are also often interested in and responsive to music. As it is both motivating and engaging, music may be used as a natural "reinforcer" for desired responses. "It's just amazing to see how music can touch children and adults, and how it can heal and make a difference in people's lives in so many different ways," said Marcia E. Humpal, former Vice President of American Music Therapy Association and current co-chair of AMTA's Autism Strategic Priority Workgroup. Through personal clinical experience, we have drawn parallels between research and clinical practice that support the value of using music therapy to address communication, social behavior, and emotional/behavioral self-regulation in individuals diagnosed with Autism and/or Alzheimer's.

Communication

While addressing communication goals with a particular seven-year-old client diagnosed with Autism and Expressive Aphasia, musical gifts were immediately recognized. Aphasia is characterized as an impairment of language ability, ranging from having difficulty remembering words to being completely unable to speak, read, or write. While this disorder can vary in presentation, through music-based activities, Neil's expressive skills and gifts surfaced. Through his involvement in music therapy, Neil was able to verbally label pitch and to demonstrate rhythmic accuracy when reading music. It was apparent through these musical experiences that a sense of emotional satisfaction for Neil and his parents had been created. This gift alone provided a bonding avenue for the child and his parents. Neil's mother and father showed increased motivation and enthusiasm in exploring effective ways to communicate with their son. As he continues to attend family music therapy sessions, Neil and his parents are both equally invested in continuing to improve communication and to further strengthen the family dynamic.

Similarly, while working on communication goals with Joe, an elderly man diagnosed with Alzheimer's, many gifts became apparent. In addition to an Alzheimer's diagnosis, Joe suffered from a stroke which left him paralyzed. Through music and other creative arts modalities, the music therapist worked to improve communication as well as strengthen rapport with his wife after medical trauma had occurred. In one particular session, Joe took much effort to communicate as he pointed to letters on a visual communication chart. Joe expressed that he was interested in being able to celebrate his anniversary with his wife. Despite his tendency to be short and easily frustrated, Joe continued to share his interests regarding his hope. Together, the music therapist and Joe decided to re-write a song which he would share with his wife on their anniversary day.

Over the next several weeks, Joe identified a special song and enthusiastically contributed lyrics, as well as concepts on how to present this gift to his wife. Just a week before his passing, Joe presented his wife with a visual print out as they listened to the song together. The gift for the music therapist was a deeper appreciation for all forms of communication and that people can grow and continue to remain connected despite their setbacks. Weeks after his passing, Joe's wife sent a letter to the nursing home expressing her deepest appreciation for a wonderful anniversary and display of their affection.

Social Behavior
Understanding and demonstrating appropriate social behaviors is a complex process for those diagnosed with Autism and Alzheimer's. Through a music therapy ensemble, adolescents struggling with inappropriate social behaviors (inappropriate comments, social withdrawal, lack of boundaries) were afforded with the gift of a shared social experience to foster their growth both musically and socially. Some of the challenges for this group included understanding social roles and responsibilities, communication limits, and inaccurate perspective taking. For example, during one particular session, one member asserted confidence with respect to a conversation involving online safety and security. This young man proceeded to share with the group *his* knowledge and understanding of what constitutes a "pervert."

As he was speaking, it was clear that other members and staff were becoming anxious, uncomfortable, and fearful of the disclosed information. This led to many questions and uncertainties within the group. This situation made it clear that a clinical session related to Internet safety and security, as well as correcting information and providing greater clarity, was necessary. While sensitively addressing the topic, so as to not demean the client's perspective and knowledge, many gifts were exchanged amongst the group and therapists. Gifts such as empathy, heightened awareness for self and other's welfare, and a serious mutual conversation about a "taboo" topics resulted. In addition to the gifts the clients clearly experienced, this situation granted the therapists with pride in knowing that their clientele stretched their abilities to new heights. It also re-awakened similar concerns and actions for the therapists, and expanded their skill set and comfort with addressing sensitive matters with clients outside of this group. Through shared music-making experiences, these adolescents, family members, and staff became empowered.

During another music therapy group at an inpatient facility, a group of elderly patients diagnosed with Alzheimer's were working on the goal of establishing and maintaining appropriate social behavior. While the majority of the group was elderly men, one particular woman was significantly younger than her fellow group members. Lynn's inappropriate social behaviors consisted of excessive use of derogatory language, sharing of delusions that involved self-harm or harm to others, and interrupting the group process by shouting out at the music therapist and other members.

After reluctantly agreeing to attend a group session, Lynn positioned herself next to the therapist and close by the piano. The music therapist implemented a group instrumental improvisation to assist members in effectively and appropriately communicating their needs within the musical structure to one another. Lynn became absorbed in the process, watching as each member was invited to join in on their percussive instrument. While she typically communicated inappropriate or discouraging words to her fellow members, Lynn took the therapist's lead as she led her up to the piano. As the other group members provided a rhythmic foundation and support, Lynn and the music therapist engaged in a piano improvisation by simply playing the black keys in an upbeat, staccato (short and detached) fashion.

Lynn's physical stature changed as she bent her knees and lightly bounced to the music while playing the piano, and a smile spread across her face. At the end of the improvisation, the group members clapped and cheered for Lynn, complimenting her courage and risk-taking within the musical experience. Lynn smiled and thanked group members, sharing about the process and joy she received from participating. While Lynn's gift was effective music-making, the therapist and fellow group members' gift was receiving appropriate social reciprocation which awarded the opportunity to experience Lynn's social strengths. Later that week, it was reported that Lynn began to increase her time spent in the lunchroom, appropriately socializing with other patients.

Emotional and Behavioral Self-Regulation
Emotional and behavioral self-regulation can be a challenging task for many children and adolescents diagnosed with an Autism Spectrum Disorder (ASD). Language deficits, the ability to mediate emotional responses, lack of control involving impulsive behaviors, and how sensory information is processed by the brain make these two forms of self-regulation a critical concept. Although some individuals with ASD learn and appear more comfortable with suppressing rather than managing negative feelings and impulsivity, there are clients who are not only comfortable but ruminate in atypical and schematic behavioral and emotional responses. For example, Craig, an eleven-year-old male who becomes obsessive and impulsive when trying to manage anxiety, fear, and other emotions.

Over the years, Craig has demonstrated behaviors such as bolting, emotional reactivity, and other impulsive responses. For example, when attempting to engage him in a structured activity, Craig will respond with a combination of dysfunctional verbal, emotional, and behavioral patterns. Despite behavioral interventions, Craig would continue to display elevated reactivity and poor self-regulation which led to inattentiveness and other anxious behaviors.

Self-regulation is the ability to evaluate one's emotions and behaviors, and to exert control by directing and regulating responses. Craig's level of self-regulation is static; at times, he demonstrates control, while at other times, Craig struggles to regulate. He will repeat the same phrase for up to 60 minutes. Although typically unresponsive to re-direction, when engaged in a music activity, Craig can be motivated to attend to task and to decrease his repetitive behaviors. This transformation is a gift awarded to the music therapists that work consistently with Craig. It offers them more patience for this particular child, and increased creativity to develop activities that practice self-regulation and stimulate learning surrounding the behavior of other clientele as well. Craig has also received gifts through this therapeutic intervention. This repetitive behavior has served as a common ground between Craig and his therapists, thus strengthening their interaction and rapport. Additionally, his coping skills have improved when he is challenged to move from preferred to non-preferred activities. Through these experiences, Craig has also developed an appreciation for music, as evidenced by his verbal requests for specific songs. His elevated affect and overall improved mood while listening to these preferred songs is a bonus as well!

Along similar lines, goals involving self-regulation became apparent when working with one elderly female patient diagnosed with Alzheimer's. It was reported that this patient had a history of extreme agitation and violent behaviors towards staff. The music therapist received a referral for this woman from her family due to her passion and profession in music performance. After reading the chart, the music therapist learned that there had been several referrals for Helen to receive music therapy, and she had refused to participate.

While on the way to see another individual, the therapist noticed Helen sitting in the hallway. The music therapist introduced herself and asked permission to come see her later. Although hesitant, Helen stated that because the music therapist reminded her of her granddaughter, that she would allow the therapist five minutes of her time. It was agreed that they would meet at 3:00 pm sharp.

At 3:00 pm, the therapist arrived at Helen's room, to her surprise, to be greeted by Helen. What began as five minutes became 30 minutes.

The music therapist continued to see Helen twice a week without much music intervention thus far. The therapist learned that Helen had been a professional violin player and that due to Alzheimer's and arthritis, she was unable to play and thus not interested in music. Using the strong rapport established between the therapist and Helen, the therapist asked permission to introduce an instrument to Helen. The next day, the therapist arrived to Helen's room with an Autoharp. Helen closely examined the instrument, and identified the flaws and drawbacks of it. Eventually and with apparent disgust on her face, Helen decided she was going to experiment with this instrument. She quickly figured out the workings of the instrument and utilized her knowledge of music to play "Amazing Grace." Helen asked the therapist to sing with her as she played the chords. When leaving her room, the therapist was met by several nurses who expressed amazement that she participated as well as transferred past learned knowledge to a novel instrument. The nurses were gifted with an experience that served to remind them why they chose the field of healthcare. As a young music therapist new to the field, this opportunity to re-acquaint Helen with music was both uplifting and affirming. Helen was re-introduced to her talent and passion for music, which served as a gift for her as she continued to reside at the nursing home.

For those who have been privileged to spend time in the presence of an individual with Alzheimer's or autism, it is evident that a gift is present in some format. It is not always easy to immediately recognize the gift, but once discovered, the person's gift can be utilized as strength for learning and growth in society. One caregiver said it this way:

"When I was encouraged by a music therapist to sing to my husband who had been lost in the fog of Alzheimer's disease for so many years, he looked at me and seemed to recognize me. On the last day of his life, he opened his eyes and looked into mine when I sang his favorite hymn. I'll always treasure that last moment we shared together. Music therapy gave me that memory, the gift I will never forget." (AMTA)

Despite struggles with communication, self-regulation, and social behavior, individuals with and without diagnoses benefit from the therapeutic relationship built between themselves and the music therapist. The consistent cycle of the music therapist building rapport with the client and motivating them to share their gifts in society comes full circle as it continues to give back as we share in giving and receiving our gifts through music.

Katie Harrill, MT-BC
Creative Arts Program Supervisor/Music Therapist
katieharrill@aol.com
412.780.5155

Kory Antonacci, MT-BC
Music Therapist
KoryAntonacci@gmail.com

Creative Journeys: Art as the Language of Dementia
Michelle Burns

I was 23 years old when my first child came into the world. It would have been impossible for me to fathom how much she would change my life forever. I never pictured myself as the motherly type. I was kind and friendly but, anything but doting. I was brutally honest with people when given the chance. I enjoyed the world and saw beauty in many things. I was naïve and sheltered and a little frightened. I was artistic but didn't know how to harness my creativity. I had been exposed to things you never want your child to know. These things made me distrusting and distant. But they also taught me to relish challenges and to be an optimist in the face of difficult circumstances. I was stubborn but happy. I was a walking, talking bundle of contradiction. And, with the birth of my daughter, about to be thrust into a world I never knew existed.

Everything changed when I was blessed with the birth of a daughter who has Down's syndrome. Either you know someone with Down's syndrome and know exactly what I'm talking about, or you don't and you think I'm a little crazy. Down's syndrome is a condition that causes, among other things, cognitive delay, and memory impairment, issues with motor skills and speech abilities, and even physical challenges. But it also includes an impeccable, if not uncanny, ability to grasp life in the moment. In my young age, I didn't really understand her limitations and proceeded to treat her as I would any child. We were learning the ropes together. Sixteen months later, I had my second child. Shortly thereafter, I became a single mother with two young children. We were all in for an amazing adventure. In fact, my younger daughter would reap benefits that she probably still doesn't appreciate. Out of necessity, she shared in her sister's early intervention that included swimming, exercise, and speech, occupational and physical therapy. Both of my children were allowed to enter pre-school at a very early age to counter any delays or risks. My younger daughter marveled at (and was somewhat jealous of) her sister's flexibility during muscle toning exercises, so we did them together, challenging our own bodies more than hers. Both of my daughters participated in Special Olympics as though they were ordinary sports teams.

Despite learning about many challenging things, (heart wrenching judgmental stares and painstaking diverging curriculum as school years past) what we learned about most was living in the moment. People are different, brains are different, and bodies are different. But, if you can master being in that very moment, suddenly you are free of the burden of expectation. Your mind is free to see beauty and kindness and give beauty and kindness in return. You are free of the constraints of time. My younger daughter grew up not understanding, or perhaps even believing in, defining people by abilities. Both of my children were open, caring and limitlessly loving to others and they taught me to live life the same way. But more than that, they taught me to be brave.

As a creative release, I delved into my art. When I would paint, my daughters would paint and we would disappear into a world where no one judged. Harsh realities softened and colors swirled together to symbolize unity. We developed the wonderful ability to let creativity speak when words couldn't. I was finally finding my artist's voice. I was also learning about using creativity and art as a tool to give someone else their voice. It didn't matter what the outcome was, the world I saw through my daughter's eyes when she was creating was perfect. Literally, a world without flaw.

I began working with inner city kids using art as a prevention method. I found this work rewarding and challenging. There was something magical that happened when you gave an angry, at risk youth a mound of malleable clay and a dose of encouragement. Something useful happened with hands that were desperately itching to find activity in sketchy surroundings. I started bringing my daughters to the studio basically because, as a single mom, I had to. I was worried about how insensitive these kids might be. They were from a world where they had often been harshly ridiculed and they knew words and laughter could sting. As the kids sat down and began creating art together, that all melted away. Rough and tumble, yet awkward, adolescent boys, tattooed at too young of an age, began showing signs of compassion.

The very same kids I had seen swaggering down the street, shouting obscenities to passing cars and sometimes engaging in quite destructive behavior, were softening. In that moment, they forgot that it might not look cool to help someone so different. I witnessed the magic of acceptance. These kids liked the art my daughter created. Her face beamed as people complimented her creations. Things were starting to click for me. Art was becoming a soulful and meaningful link for people where before, there had been none. I was also starting to see that I could level the playing field by modifying projects to allow creativity to be equally interesting even if the ability wasn't the same. We didn't focus on technical skills but instead on the vast and mysterious vision in drawing, painting or sculpting. We explored the freedom of abstract art and impressionism and meaning that was not so literal. We explored viewing creativity as a voice without defining "correctness."

The same time that I was working with inner city kids, I began volunteering with the Alzheimer's Association as an art facilitator with people who had Alzheimer's disease. This represented a new group of people to work with and I found it surprisingly comfortable. I received training through the Memories in the Making program which primarily used water color paintings inspired by photographs. I would arrive at various facilities to set up the room for our painting sessions and then the staff would bring people to the room to engage in artistic expression. This was where I first learned specific practical techniques to aid in the creative process. The most helpful was using painter's tape to create a border around the watercolor paper and actually tape the whole piece to the table. This allowed the artist to paint without having to hold the paper still.

After four years of working in these two related, but very different fields, I found I was spread too thin. I felt the need to focus my efforts and hone my skills in one specific field. I was also ready for a geographical change. Colorado had been home for most of my life and it was time for something new. I began searching for positions in the San Francisco Bay area in California. I sent my resume out and received several very appealing responses including one from Senior Access Adult Day Center working as the Activity Director with people who had a diagnosis of dementia. After a few emails, I had an interview set up and a plane ticket in hand.

My interview was exciting and seemed like the perfect fit. Jen Tripathy was the Program Director and as she showed me around the building, she introduced me to members of the program. I found myself inspired but, I also saw the challenges. This was a program that members came to, not a facility that they lived in. This meant 5 hours a day of focused, energy filled, non-stop activity. This activity needed to be engaging, but balanced, so it was not overwhelming or over stimulating. Also, the range of abilities and needs of our members was very broad. Some had dementia, some had physical challenges and some had psychiatric issues. Some had all three or a combination of these issues. This was a state licensed facility that required reporting and record keeping. The regulations were clear and strict in terms of the care provided and documenting legal compliance. These administrative duties were comprehensive and time consuming and filled the other 3 hours of my day. I wanted to somehow mold what I had learned about the magic of art into this program. Achieving my goals for the program while fulfilling the administrative duties would be a long and curvy road.

The idea of art as a therapeutic activity for those with Alzheimer's was just starting to emerge. Some people regarded this as groundbreaking, innovative and useful. Most, however, where still looking for scientifically proven techniques and saw art strictly as a "busy-time" craft activity. Even my staff was overwhelmed at, and resistant to, the thought of participating in creative projects with our members. Facilitating these projects necessitated hands on assistance. This would prove to be a large component in the success of moving our art program forward. Luckily, Jen, our very progressive Program Director, was on my side. She was a fellow artist and loved the thought of doing something really unique in the field. She has gone to battle for me many times and was my first strong ally. She supported and implemented adding the component of assisting with art activities to our staff's written job descriptions. This was controversial, to say the least. After all, didn't these under-recognized, hands-on program assistants already have enough to do? These are people (along with other staff members) that I admire every day and to whom I owe a debt of gratitude.

After the dust of these changes settled, I began assessing the environment. I started by throwing all the crayons away. These were adults and surely there must be a way to use artist's materials in a safe way. I explored relatively simple art projects that I thought would be interesting for our staff as well as engaging for our members. For example, colored pencil art is calming and allows practice in fine motor skills. This is something that many of our members hadn't done in years. Putting pencil to paper utilized spatial awareness, decision making and the, seemingly simple, skill of holding a pencil. I recognized that age appropriate projects were also paramount. When providing care for someone that has diminished or changing cognitive abilities, there may be a natural inclination to use overly simplified projects. It was important to offer something that would present a tranquil activity without insulting our member's adult sensibility. Coloring mandala patterns quickly became a favorite. These are circular shapes with repeating geometric patterns used in Eastern religions to represent wholeness. Their history is long and provides a back story that is anything but childish. Most of all, they provided an activity for a very broad range of needs and abilities. Our members became so adept at decorating their mandalas; they later became the inspiration for a beautiful stained glass art piece that was presented to us by a local artist.

Once I felt acclimated with my administrative duties, I was ready to branch out with more complex projects. I knew attention needed to be paid to the many complications that would present themselves when working in this field. Confusion may lead to accidental ingestion of materials, a project that was too complex could quickly be rejected, and the length of a project was an issue. Activities that extended beyond thirty minutes could be very tiring for our members, both physically and mentally. I searched many books and websites for ideas. We started with projects that were more craft than art but, on the whole, were successful with our members. They inspired participation and conversation and the program staff was happy to see finished pieces being displayed. For the first time, other administrative staff began seeing the merit in this creative work with our members. An autumn Senior Fair was approaching and we thought it might be a great promotional idea to present something that people could take home with them. We agreed on a handcrafted piece of art that was attractive to people in the community. I had been actively changing our projects to create things a little more outside the box and this would be our initial public unveiling.

After a lot of consideration, I thought it would be fun to create place card or photo holders using square wooden cubes with a wire holder extending from the top. This was not a particularly unique notion, but what would make the cubes interesting was decorating them with trinkets of the member's choosing. We used everything from marbles to scrabble pieces. The cubes became small treasure chests that told stories about each member. Some were practical and systematic like carefully patterned mosaics. Some were free and loose like fanciful jars of candy. Every cube (150 in all) was unique and intriguing. You couldn't help but hold them and explore their stories. What was most amazing about the project was how much our members relished the creative time spent on them. There were days that we joked about breaking out the cubes again, but every time, every day was a new adventure. If I presented a project or message with confidence and exuberance, members were happy to oblige. The facilitator's delivery is a very big part of succeeding with this type of program.

The cubes were wildly popular and we sold many as a fundraiser. This fed the fire in me. I was ready to start looking for creative projects beyond craft ideas that were growing tired and over used. I enjoyed the challenge of modifying creative steps, while ensuring interesting, more sophisticated outcomes. I was also longing for that moment of triumph I felt while watching my daughter proudly connect with someone through her art. That moment when ability was less important and art became its own magical, uninhibited language.

During conversations with visitors to our program, they often responded with surprise to learn that someone with dementia had created a piece that was on display. This would be a repeating theme for the coming years and one that inspired me to keep forging ahead. At first, I was a little insulted at the surprised reactions. *I* fully understood that our members were capable of creating appealing artwork and thought it was ignorant for people to not see beyond stereotypes. I wasn't quite sure how to respond to my feelings and then started to understand where I was in my world. I had spent the last 16 years seeing the beautiful art my daughter created while battling judgment from others. I spent the last 4 years working with people whose entire personalities, and certainly their abilities, had changed beyond recognition for their loved ones. I had a lot of time to develop acceptance and equip myself for these challenges. I cherished my time with our members and I knew I was the lucky one that saw them where they were now, not ten years ago. This knowledge also came with a large responsibility. I had to use my personal experiences to tread lightly in communication. I reveled in victory when a member could complete a simple watercolor painting of a flower and it didn't even occur (or matter) to me that this same person used to be a doctor. Not only did I need to be ever present in how I spoke to the member but I also needed to honor their spouses, children, and caregivers who were mourning the loss of this person. On some level, I even knew how they felt. Despite my endless efforts to raise my daughter as a typical child, I heard people's comments. I knew people felt sorry for me that my child was different and my life would forever be bound to her in a manner very different than with other children. I knew people from the outside thought our life was difficult and challenging and, sometimes it was. But, it was also difficult and challenging with my other daughter. Raising children is difficult and challenging.

Yes, these people had changed. Wives who had depended on their husbands for 50 years for support and love had to face the reality that this was a fading recognition. Children who were protected by their parents now had to take care of them as though they were the youngsters. Who cares if they could color a picture or glue a bobble onto a cube? But, what started happening was that these spouses, children and caregivers saw something change. Members would arrive home tired, but satisfied. They wanted to talk about something they had done that day, something they had created. Sometimes, people could not find the words to talk about the day, but they were happy. Something was resonating. I started to see that I was making a *choice* to see people in a different way and that this choice was making a huge difference. It gave them a new voice. I wanted to use this creative expression, this voice, to demonstrate the gifts of being in the moment *with* Alzheimer's disease. This presented a difficult message to swallow. The reality of this new voice was sometimes frightening and challenging, but also a magical rush of pure and poignant discovery.

Family members would come to our program to witness this creative process and see just what all the fuss was about. They saw that we spoke to our members in a deliberate tone. We never complained about something they couldn't do, or pointed out that something was childish or simple. We spoke with a respectful tone and patiently gave gentle verbal directions in easy to follow steps. They saw that we talked about age appropriate and relevant subjects. They saw that we were using our activities to reach out to them where they were, not expecting them to meet us where we were. They saw that we were using art to bridge a gap. Art was opening people up—they were telling stories about their lives, their losses and their dreams. They were showing this through their creation. We joked and laughed and, most importantly, we never scolded when people repeated themselves. A common teaching tool that I use in working with people with Alzheimer's or dementia is to treat each conversation as though it is the first time we have ever spoken on that subject. This rule was also true for creating art. Steps would need to be repeated many, many times over. Because of the clearly evident excitement, staff rarely minded this. Members would sometimes become frustrated and needed a moment to stop working and that was okay. Most of the time, they would see their neighbor still working away and they would be drawn back into their art.

Through these projects, what I observed was a growing sense of pride. This was a long lost sensation for many of our members. Again, I found myself wanting to go further. At this same time, Cris Chater, our Executive Director was eager to effect another change. She had a vision to change the language we used to talk about those with dementia altogether. She had the support of Dr. Pat Fox, a member of our Advisory Council and Co-director of the Institute on Health and Aging at University of California San Francisco. Dr. Fox had recently shared a paper he co-authored about reframing how we look at "forgetfulness" to see the blessings of these people rather than the loss. This was exhilarating to me as it spoke to the very core of my beliefs. We started to brainstorm about creating a paradigm shift. Instead of "client" we would say "member", instead of "program" we would say "club". We had monthly calendars hanging up, but we didn't focus on what the day or date was. If someone wanted to know, we would tell them but, I didn't even want to be reminded of how quickly time was passing, why would they? With the guidance of Cris, the program challenged itself daily to upgrade our performance on ethical issues and best practices. We were all working to be in the moment. We were truly living in the present. Cris revamped our entire information program to envision an exclusive club for those with memory loss. Our staff would create a new reality upon entering our building, a sanctuary with no constraints of time. Wherever our members were in the moment, that's where we would be with them.

When talking about my art program or projects, I use the term "artist" because that is how we have defined our practice. The completed art projects were nicely framed and hung on the wall and displayed like a true piece of art. I was taken back to the days with my daughter when the world was perfect when we created art together. The playing field was beginning to be leveled. Even when members couldn't remember creating a piece of art, they would recognize color, texture, and sometimes a deeply personal message. They would comment on how beautiful a piece was and when we reminded them that they had created it, they first blushed and then grinned in accomplishment. These artists were releasing themselves into an unexplored world and loving it. Freedom of expression became our mantra and the facets of our program became an exciting and magical concoction.

I also witnessed more changes. Members that first came to our program agitated and anxious were growing. They were able to engage for longer periods of time, their confidence was increasing and peer interaction was emerging. Where it was once difficult to sit still for a 5 minute project, now 45 minutes disappeared to creativity. Reluctant artists that once hesitated to hold a brush were mixing bold, vibrant silk dyes together. Art became a catalyst for people who were desperately missing conversation with someone their own age. They found friends to laugh and reminisce with in sharing their discoveries. Their presence in the moment provided an exciting perspective on life. Struggles became opportunities and, more than that, they became gifts.

Our art projects became more "artistically" driven and the outcomes became wildly interesting. We delved into collage, sculpture, and painting. Some of our projects were not always attractive, but they were always intriguing. I was able to use what I had learned about modifying projects into simple steps to ensure that the finished pieces looked like sophisticated art. Even I was amazed at the outcomes and we ventured into more and more creative realms. Nothing was too much of a challenge as we conquered silk painted banners, huge multi-media canvases, and interesting textile pieces. One of our more memorable projects was making prints using real (dead) fish and printer's ink. Again, this was not a new concept in art, but for this population, it was. This provided hours of storytelling and a wonderful sense of adventure for our members. These projects continued to build a sense of accomplishment, confidence and laughter. Members began to trust the many crazy things I brought to them and they would chuckle when I would praise their creative color choices or provocative collage photos. What once took significant coaxing and explanation now saw artists diving right in. Our program had become a true art class - a carefully orchestrated and modified course in creativity for people with memory loss.

I have been unquestionably fortunate in my work. I've presented at conferences, local and abroad, about the philosophy of my art program. I've taught workshops to other professionals as well as caregivers and I've worked with students at local universities to further our philosophy. I have curated several public exhibits to share our member's remarkable artwork. Perhaps, what I'm most proud of is our efforts to change the stigma and fear of Alzheimer's disease through awareness and education. I have relied on art to bridge this gap and to create the Holding Time Bowl Initiative. This project was developed to provide a non-threatening way to demystify the ever changing world of our artists. By sharing a series of intriguing pieces, we could draw people into this journey and the magical transformations that creativity provides. Artists used a series of 6 different types of bowls of varying weight, capacity, texture and function to emulate the stages of memory loss. The mediums ranged from solid and opaque to light and flexible. As a metaphor to the human mind, this change in medium demonstrated the change in ability to hold things – in this case, memory. It showed that memory was not the sole measure of meaning. These bowls also told a story about the gifts that remain and the gifts that have *emerged* in this enlightening stage of our artist's lives.

While it is somewhat unorthodox to correlate "gifts" with a degenerative affliction such as Alzheimer's disease, I hope that my work can provide testimony that these gifts do, in fact, exist. The remarkable stories and pieces our artist's share, provide a voice from within - a voice that too often goes unheard. This is not a science, it is human. It is the very core of what gives us faith that we can persevere. That there can be quality in life and adaption to circumstance and most of all, the elusive unconditional acceptance we all seek and deserve. I often wonder if I will face the proverbial coming of full circle in my life. Will my daughter be one of the likely people with Down's syndrome to develop Alzheimer's disease? Although statistically, the answer is yes, these are the questions I don't have answers to. But what I do know is that I was forever changed by what she taught me about being in the moment. About bravely facing down skepticism and being open to surprising abilities when we had become so focused on seeing inability or loss. Yes, I have been tested to the point where, if given the choice, I might have opted for an easier path. But, because of the invaluable lessons from my daughter and the people I work with, I can now face these uncertainties knowing about and believing in these gifts.

Michelle Burns, chiliwack36@yahoo.com

I would not paint a face, a rock, nor brooks, nor trees. Mere semblances of things, but something more than these.

That art is best to which the soul's range gives no bound. Something besides the form, something beyond the sound.

Anonymous
8th Century

A Clowns-Eye-View of Things: Reflections on a theater program for people with special needs
Naree Shields

Over the past three years I have been creating theater with people who have special needs. The groups consist of people with various forms of autism, down syndrome, physical disabilities, sight, hearing and voice impairments. Often I don't know specifically what the "disability" is, but I know that extraordinary moments happen in our time together; I call these "Standing Ovation moments" and they illustrate that autism and other disabilities do have positive aspects. Perhaps the most notable gift is the opportunity to see and experience reality in a myriad of ways.

Often the behaviors I see amongst people with special needs are very clown like:

> *"A clown does whatever they want, wherever they want, for as long as they want."* Ira Seidenstein

Clowning is very much about being fully present in the moment. In my own study of clowns and observations from teaching, I contemplate:

> *What does it feel like to be able to allow yourself to surrender into a depth of feeling where the body is charged and the imagination fired up? Is it possible to find peace and grace in this state?*

In 2012 I facilitated a 6 month project with adults called "All things Clown." In weekly workshops we played together and I directed a couple of performance pieces that were performed and received by the audience with much delight.

This simple scenario is a classic slapstick style routine with Charlie Chaplin music being played in the background where one of the actors was mostly non-verbal. It relishes in simplicity and embellishing mundane moments. In directing this routine I was putting a frame around authentic qualities and feelings that revealed themselves in our workshops. I wanted the sage-like quality of stillness to be seen.

This theatrical skit gave the audience a way of seeing authentic qualities whilst experiencing the participants in a positive and joyous way.

Through facilitating these workshops I have witnessed that there are diverse ways of knowing and understanding the world. It is enriching to work with all the different textures that this diversity contains. For a six-month period in one of my classes, Jerome always ran into the class and went to his spot near the piano. He always stood outside the circle and rocked. When we said good morning around the circle, Mike would always get up from his seat and go over to Jerome and connect his elbow with Jerome's and say, "Good morning Jerome, good morning." Throughout the class Jerome would make an extraordinary soundscape whilst continuing to rock. I noticed that the quality of the sounds would change depending on the type of energy that was in the space. It seemed that the soundscape was like an emotional barometer. I mused that Jerome should be present in a parliamentary meeting to be an integrity barometer—to help people be more aware of what was truly taking place beyond the socially accepted exchanges in communication. I find it enriching to spend time with people who do not conform to normal ways of being and encourage me to expand my horizon of understanding the world.

I have learned a lot about spaciousness, flexibility and trust in this work. I have had to slow down my pace in order to become more in-tune with what is really taking place in each moment. This act of slowing down has been an extraordinarily transformative teaching for me, and enabled me to become more connected with myself and others; the effects have rippled into all aspects of my life.

I have also learned to be OK with not knowing exactly what the outcome of the work will look like. There is a clear structure in terms of a particular sequence of games and activities. However, there is a spirit of flexibility to respond according to what is coming up in the space each moment. For example, in my Friday class we are in the middle of an activity and Mickey enters the space because he feels like doing the "happy dance"—joining hands with a partner and jump his heels together. When Mickey first did this I said, "Yes" to see what might happen by exploring this offer. As a result, the "happy dance" has become a regular happening in our class and it was written into our "Cinderella" show that we created 2 years ago. In this show my colleague and I performed alongside clients and careers. This performance received a standing Ovation; there was so much energy and joy present. I think telling stories is a built-in part of our human DNA. People thrive when they get to share their stories, and the stories can be told in a myriad of ways including through gesture, dance, sound, silence, stillness.

Like alchemy, in our workshops many things are put into the pot and worked with. Through time and a quality of mind that allows things to be exactly as they are, a distillation takes place. The attributes of the gold include:

- Positive feelings and a sense of well-being.
- The cultivation of enhanced relationships of self and other (Including richer interactions between participants and career's).
- A new sense of confidence in participants with a more positive perception of self.
- An enhanced ability to interact and work collaboratively with others.
- An opportunity for people to see each other in new ways.

The key ingredients in this process are a light-hearted and playful approach. In one of my high school groups, I started to notice through the clowning exercises that Frieda, a young woman with down syndrome and a selective mute, delighted in being naughty. Clowning is a wonderful tool for exploring mischief and socially unacceptable behaviors.

Frieda began to whisper knock knock jokes in class. It was reported that she told her "nick off" joke to the principal, and at the age of 10 at her retreat, she told a joke into a microphone in front of her peers! Most of her peers had never heard her speak a word. I consider this a standing ovation moment and an illustration that a light-hearted approach has medicinal qualities. I have noticed that anxiety is a major player in the lives of these kids. But drawing on my own experience I know that if the space is safe and it is held with an awareness that encompasses kindness, then all manner of possibilities reveal themselves.

Another important key is to honor each person's process and innate timing. J.D, a participant in my Friday class, mostly sits outside the circle in class and for the first 18 months would not participate in activities. One day, I asked J.D if she would like to do a funny walk across our acting space. J.D stood up and did an outrageous walk. This was most unexpected but received with so much enthusiasm by everybody who was witnessing this standing ovation moment.

Not long after this, J.D brought in a script that she had written, "Vampires of New York." This became the play that we performed at the end of last year. J.D was the story teller on stage, in front of hundreds of people. Just as flowers bloom, people bloom when the conditions are right. And I like to think that weeds are also a type of flower- weeds are simply more unconventional and labeled differently.

"You show me how a wild flower grows and I'll tell you what a clown is" ~ Ira Seidenstein.

I love that the theatre making process offers the opportunity to share meaningful moments with people from diverse backgrounds. Especially when approached with light-heartedness, it provides a place to play and explore aspects of our shared humanity.

I have been enriched and gifted through my work with people with autism. I am deeply grateful for the continued opportunity to keep opening my heart and mind to new ways of seeing and being.

Naree Shields, New Whales Australia
clownmedicine@gmail.com
Naree is a freelance teacher and theater maker and has been mentored by Dr. Ira Seidenstine. Naree has facilitated theater programs for students with disabilities throughout Australia

CHAPTER 6

Establishing Rapport & Cultivating an Atmosphere of Trust, Unconditional Love, Acceptance, & Self-Determination

In the early 1970s when I was on my spiritual quest for self-rehabilitation and self-empowerment, I discovered the importance of self-esteem and self-worth.

Two books in particular were instrumental in shaping my career: *Summerhill* by A.S. Neil, a book about a "free school" in England, and *No Language But a Cry* by Dr. Richard Ambrosio, a true story about a orphaned girl who had been beaten consistently and severely burned over most of her body, including her face. The subject of the book was horrifically traumatized in her young life, causing her profound depression and a complete withdrawal from the external world.

Summerhill was instrumental in helping me understand the importance of self-esteem and the value of a free (that is, less structure- and rule-driven), loving environment for raising and educating children.

Ambrosio's book, *No Language But a Cry*, detailed his unwavering persistence and patience as he worked with the young girl to establish rapport and cultivate a trusting relationship characterized by unconditional love and acceptance. After five years of gentle and loving care, Dr. Ambrosio's little patient started to talk and eventually, with plastic surgery to fix her disfigured face in tandem with Ambrosio's compassionate therapy, she was able to return to the community.

The common message I took from these books—about loving, rapport-focused, empowering, and trusting care—would be the philosophical foundation of my life and an abundantly fulfilling career.

Nurturing and Self-Empowerment
In my opinion, many of our current social and perhaps economic problems could be solved with the following:
- Nurturing parents and educators, and administrators
- Self-esteem and self-reliance
- Allowing children and individuals self-direction, self-responsibility, authentic power, unconditional love, unconditional valuing, and unconditional acceptance.

Critics argue that such self-focused philosophical practices are simplistic and urge applying more sophisticated theories, methodologies, and practices. The more "sophisticated" methods often relied on behavioral modification and detailed behavior plans, which in my observation and experience, created more behaviors than they corrected.

In my opinion, the more practical and traditional approaches are driven primarily by fear and the desire to make a system more complicated for financial gain. How nurturing were your parents or teachers? Were you urged to find your own voice with loving acceptance, or were your academic and life lessons based on expectations and rules? Historically, in a patriarchal and success-oriented culture as we've found in the United States for the last century (or more), those who are in charge of us and our upbringing have directed us down "tried and true" paths. It's not that they did not care about us—but based on their own fears for our well-being and their understanding of "what works," they perhaps unknowingly stifled us and our personal paths and destinies.

Success with the Arts
In the early 1970s I was able to try out my philosophical ideals by selling the Summerhill concept to my colleagues at one of the first regional high school's in the country for people with physical disabilities in Dayton, Ohio. I replicated the free school approach exemplified in the book by encouraging a joyful, playful, and productive learning environment.

The students helped develop the types of classes they wished to take. Because the students designed their own classes based on their interests, the teachers likewise felt empowered to teach academics relevant to their students. All of the academic classes were extremely practical and functional for what students needed for the "real world." Students also benefited from a weekly peer counseling support group session.

It was at this school that I first witnessed the powerful benefits of music, art, and theatre for individuals with disabilities. I started a theatre class where the students wrote and performed in a weekly production of their own "As the Wheels Turn" soap opera. I could write a book on all of the objectives that this activity fulfilled (and I might!). The students could not wait to come to school to engage themselves in their brilliant performances and view the videotapes of their dramas.

The creativity and self-expression they were allowed not only afforded them enjoyment, but also immensely enhanced their self-esteem, self-worth, and self-confidence.

I spent ten joyful years at the school, but I left when the administration started to impose required curricula with grading requirements. I later learned that the students didn't have as much fun and lacked the motivation to learn.

Although you may agree that a focus on nurturing the individual is common sense stuff, can be a successful approach, and should be easy to do, try implementing it in a rule-driven bureaucratic world!

***

Using lessons derived from *No Language But a Cry*, I applied play therapy at Dayton's Children's Hospital where I volunteered in 1975. A friend who worked at a local parent's anonymous chapter approached me to conduct play therapy for children who had been abused or neglected. Most of the children in the group were either hyperactive or withdrawn. My first mission was to establish rapport and cultivate a loving and safe environment for these kids, who were generally starved for love, acceptance, and attention.

One five-year-old I recall particularly was very withdrawn because of previous emotional, physical, and sexual abuse. Her father was in prison, and her mother was intellectually challenged. Working one-on-one with her slowly and cautiously using puppets, I came to earn her trust. Much like a caterpillar transforming into a magnificent butterfly, this child grew and began interacting with the other children as she felt increasingly safe and able to trust.

Tragically, one day, I was informed that this little girl was critically injured when her mother's boyfriend and her older siblings forced her into a tub of scalding hot water that had been prepared for her. This was when I stopped this program—frankly, I felt discouraged and heartbroken working with children who would be returned to abusive situations. I believed more than ever that nurturing and love and allowing self-expression are critical for healing at-risk children or any disenfranchised inviduals.

***

Another example from my early career of the benefits of music and the arts is my experience as a transportation supervisor for persons with disabilities. I had difficulty maintaining a driver for a particularly chaotic route that consisted of mostly autistic children, so I decided to try something different, and I drove the route myself. I brought a cassette tape player with me when I drove and played what some may call "elevator music." Not only was the music calming and soothing to the individuals aboard the bus, but it produced a more relaxed collective environment as well.

During the drive to school, the children would rock themselves and be pacified by the music. I felt the music strategy was very successful, until I received a call from the special education director regarding concerns from several teachers that in encouraging the rocking and self-soothing, I was reinforcing "socially unacceptable behavior." Remember, though, that in the early 1970s, it was the practice of many teachers to use water bottles and restraints and even pepper on tongues to eliminate such behaviors as rocking.

Fortunately, we all have learned much about autism since then, and teachers and other professionals are understanding how to structure an environment to meet the needs of autistic individuals and are learning how to proactively redirect behaviors and prevent disruptive or harmful behaviors.

The Advent of Normalization and "Gentle Teaching"

The demystification period of the 1980s in particular afforded persons with disabilities the opportunity to move out of institutions and back into their communities. Unfortunately, much of the time, they were still treated much as they had been in institutions. However, leaders in the field of disabilities at this time started to educate staff and families about "normalization" and empowering persons with disabilities. Many methods and practices tried during this period were based on the principles of Wolf Wolfensberger, an American academic who championed the European concept of normalization of those with disabilities.

For me, it was so refreshing to discover in 1990 the work of Dr. John McGee, who had packaged a system he called "gentle teaching," an innovative approach that is much like the self-empowering and nurturing concepts I discuss in this chapter as well as in the chapter called "Behavior is Language."

According to various websites on the subject, gentle teaching focuses on teaching four essential feelings to the individuals who are served: safe, love, loving, and engaged. Caregivers not only need to ensure that those who are served are safe, but more importantly, feel safe! This gentle, loving way of engaging and interacting with all people—but especially those who have been marginalized and disenfranchised—brought me so much success in the two decades before I personally met Dr. McGee, as well as in the subsequent decades.

Since my early career, I believe that we as a society and we who care for and educate persons with disabilities have made significant progress in the areas of self-determination, consumer choice, and person-centered planning and practices.

Most agencies today profess these concepts, however not all "walk the walk." In geriatrics, especially in nursing homes and assisted living, such person-centered concepts are still in their infancy. For example, while my mother was living in assisted living, she had a cherished doll that she believed to be real. This doll was her lifeline, and to her, it was like one of her own children. She would talk to it, nurture it, cuddle it, and play with it. If you wanted to take it from her so she could eat or attend to other business, she would become agitated.

During one such time when a caretaker was trying to give her medication, my mother did not want her doll (child) taken from her. A struggle ensued, and the caretaker took the doll, saying my mother could not have it back until she took the medicine. Mom became very angry, rightfully so—her child had just been taken from her!— she cursed (out of character for her), kicked, and tried to bite the caretaker. I happened to walk in during the struggle and was able to redirect my mother, turning her attention to something else until she calmed.

Person-Centered Care and Dementia
The various paradigm shifts that attempt to put the person first versus a focus on the system are finally becoming more popular within the geriatric care community.

Dr. Timothy Epp, is his 2003 article "Person-centered Dementia Care: A Vision to be Refined," characterizes well the state of dementia care in the late 1990s and early in the new century. He acknowledges that "while the person- or consumer-centered approach to care had been used successfully for persons with disabilities, we understand less about its application and implementation in dementia care settings."[1] In his article, Dr. Epp reviews the literature to that point, quoting other experts to hypothesize on the application of such care to those with dementia:

"Person-centered dementia care (PCC) has emerged as a response to an old culture of care which: 1) reduced dementia to a strictly biomedical phenomenon; 2) was task-driven; 3) relied on control techniques including chemical and physical restraints, warehousing, and unnecessary medication; and 4) devalued the agency and individuality of person with dementia. In contrast, PCC is value-driven, focuses on independence, well-being, and empowerment of

---

1 Epp, Timothy. "Person-centered Dementia Care: A Vision to be Refined." *Canadian Alzheimer's Disease Review.* (2003): 14-18. Print.

individuals and families, 'and enables the person to feel supported, valued, and socially confident.' Promotion of PCC also is a response to the lack of attention in dementia research and to the agency and subjectivity of persons with dementia."[2]

Despite the research and insights by Dr. Epp and others studying the care dynamic of adults with dementia, my visits to various nursing homes and assisted-living facilities over the years are indicative of the ongoing desperate need for reforming systems and facility structures themselves—and for more aggressive transformation of staff training to value residents' "independence, well-being, and empowerment."[3]

In their 2009 article on person-centered care (as well as the need to "reconceptualize the meaning of Alzheimer's disease"), Shabahangi, Faustman, and Geoffrey call for a "reorganization of the social typing of people with Alzheimer's to be more inclusive of the notion of personhood."[4] The authors also ask that "we as a society temper the demonization of the disease so we don't lose sight of our social responsibility to care for people with dementia in ways that recognize and preserve their dignity as human beings. Such efforts are already underway as models of person-centered, relationship-centered, and family-centered care begin to emerge for persons with Alzheimer's."

This "expansion of the clinical gaze has implications for caregiving, if for no other reason than we will have more and more people labeled with the diagnosis for longer periods of their life than ever before. This raises the important question of what does the forgetful person bring to our lives? This question is often put aside in the attempt to understand the disease at the expense of the person who has the disease."

Dr. Epp, in his person-centered article, cites other studies discussing self-esteem and its value in dementia cases. PCC involves establishing and maintaining positive, supportive, social environments for persons with dementia. In these contexts, personhood of individuals with dementia may be enhanced by strengthening the person's positive feelings, nurturing the person's abilities or skills, and helping the healing of a psychic wound.

A favorite wisdom of mine regarding positive interactions with persons in dementia care comes from Dr. Epp's article (adapted from the work of T. Kitwood), which he expresses in the following table:[5]

2 Ibid.
3 Ibid.
4 Shabahangi, Nader, Geoffrey Faustman, et al. "Some Observations on the Social Consequences of Forgetfulness and Alzheimer's Disease: A Call for Attitudinal Expansion." *Journal of Aging, Humanities, and the Arts.* 3. (2009): 38-52. Print.
5 Epp, Timothy. "Person-centered Dementia Care: A Vision to be Refined." *Canadian Alzheimer's Disease Review.* (2003): 14-18. Print.

Recognition   Individual is known as a unique person by name: involves verbal communicating and eye contact.

Negotiation   Individual is consulted about preferences, choice, needs.

Collaboration   Caregiver aligns him/herself with care recipient to engage in a task.

Play   Encouraging expressions of spontaneity and of self.

Stimulation   Engaging in interactions using senses.

Celebration   Celebrating anything the individual finds enjoyable.

Relaxations   Providing close personal comfort (e.g., holding hands).

Validations   Acknowledging individual's emotions and feelings and responding to them; empathy.

Holding   Providing a space where the individual feels comfortable in self-revelation.

Facilitation   Enabling individual to use his or her remaining abilities; not emphasizing errors.

Creation   Individual spontaneously offers something to the interaction; affirmation of this interaction.

Giving   Individual offers him/herself in a positive emotional or helpful way.

As Dr. Epp has said, "The future practice and development of PCC depends on several requirements. Care providers must be aware of their own values in forming their definition of 'personhood,' how these values form the practice of caring, and the fact that definitions of PCC vary among administrative personnel, front-line nursing staff, family caregivers, and the individuals with dementia themselves. Care providers must also carefully assess the factors which promote and impede PCC and share their success stories with other care providers. Academic research can also support these goals—particularly qualitative research, which applies to the experiences of dementia and caring and to the perspectives of all involved in the caring process."[6]

---

6 Ibid.

CHAPTER 7

Behavior Is Language

In my 40 years of working with people with disabilities, particularly those with autism, I have discovered that they often use behavior rather than words to express themselves. When I conduct national training workshops for teachers and care providers of persons with disabilities, I stress that even non-verbal people communicate through their behavior and body language—and that their behavior can help those around them interpret what they are trying to communicate.

Individuals with autism and Alzheimer's alike communicate through their behavior to express a feeling, need, or request and will often display abnormal responses to sensations, people, objects, and events. Striking or biting oneself or others, rocking, and loud vocalizations are common reactions of autistic persons to stressful circumstances or unpleasant sensory input, whether from noise, or taste, or tactile discomfort. What the world may call "unacceptable behavior" is often the only means by which autistic individuals or persons with dementia might be able to express their discomfort, pain, or preference.

As the previous chapter emphasized, we must create an environment where those with autism or Alzheimer's feel harmonious and safe. A positive and engaging attitude establishes an excellent rapport with a student/consumer with a disability and fosters a trusting bond. I have used the following questioning model in my workshops to illustrate that behavior is language and to engage participants in interpreting non-verbal requests, feelings, and self-stimulating behaviors:

Ask yourself:
- What is the person's behavior telling you?
- What statement or request is the person making?

What is the behavior a request for?
- Attention?
- Social interaction?
- Escape from a situation?
- To be left alone?
- Refusal?
- Information/Clarification?
- Affection?
- Objects?
- Food?
- Assistance?

What feelings are being expressed?
- Anticipation?
- Fear?
- Pleasure/Joy?
- Pain?
- Boredom?

- Hurt?
- Confusion?
- Frustration?
- Anger?
- Love/Compassion?

What self-stimulation behavior might be involved?
- Sensory Stimulation?
- Ritualistic Behavior?

Person-Centered, Empowered Care

In 1990, as executive director and CEO of a residential and employment services non-profit agency, I developed supported living and employment opportunities based on such a person-centered and empowerment-based model that I discussed in the last chapter. We would serve only those people with either medical or behavioral challenges no one else would serve, most of whom were autistic or had experienced traumatic brain injuries.

While working at this agency and conducting *Behavior is Language* workshops nationwide, I encountered several individuals whose eventual success epitomizes the effectiveness of person-centered, empowering, environmentally friendly, safe, and loving arrangements. Their stories follow (their names have been changed to preserve anonymity).

John

One of our agency's first clients, John, was not autistic, but had spent three months in a coma after suffering a Traumatic Brain Injury (TBI) fresh out of high school after skidding off an icy, snow-covered road into a utility pole.

The Brain Injury Association has defined TBI as an alteration in brain functions or other evidence of brain pathology caused by an external force. TBI seems to share characteristics with Alzheimer's, including memory and concentration problems, sensitivity to light or sound, mood changes or mood swings, profound confusion, loss of coordination, and sudden impulsivity.

Like those with Alzheimer's, John (and many people like John) could not remember much about his past. Sadly, his behavioral outbursts and impulsivity had caused him to be moved out of 20 nursing homes in 12 years. As with Alzheimer's families, the families and loved ones of TBI individuals often remark, "He is like a completely different and new person."

John's mother, Joann, was one of our agency's first board members, and upon observing the success we were having with young adults with autism, she literally begged me to help get her son out of his emotional and (sometimes literal) bondage. Joann told me that John was often placed on locked floors with schizophrenic residents and, at times, was restrained in a straightjacket. Joann was frequently making eight-hour round trips driving from Cincinnati to Cleveland to visit her son, and the family was overwhelmed.

In determining how to best handle John's situation, I asked Joann and John's social worker to describe the behaviors that had prompted his having to move out of the 20 previous nursing homes. His impulsivity and response to living in a restrictive environment with sometimes impatient or hostile employees (and perhaps with hostile residents) was not conducive to his well-being.

In a typical nursing home, John was not allowed to make many choices, and the nursing home staff often limited any preferences. For example, John said on many beautiful weekend days, he would lie in bed until noon or later because the home had not scheduled enough staff to attend to residents. John shared that often when he would ask an orderly to help him to the bathroom, he would be told "in a minute," but that minute would become minutes and then hours, and then finally, when approached, John would have had an accident. In frustration, he would impulsively hit a staff member or even rip their clothes.

I agreed to take John out of the distant nursing home, and I placed him in a supported living home, which had been modified to be accessible to his wheel chair. In his new home, John had been given the opportunity to choose his roommate and participate in interviewing the staff. He was empowered to say what he wanted and could make decisions and choices he had previously not been allowed. As a result of more freedom and increased respect for his preferences, his impulsivity and the related behaviors occurred less and less.

***

John's experience and my own feelings and observations about an education system that restricts personal growth and autonomy motivated me to commit to being an agent in transforming historically authoritative, hierarchical institutions based on fear and rigid rules and regulations that are more file- and money-driven than consumer-driven. I often felt powerless being witness to so many lives being damaged or denied opportunities to thrive.

Our agency had much success taking people with TBI out of nursing homes and serving them in homes where you or I would live. Looking back, I am struck by and amazed at the behavioral similarities between those suffering from TBI and those with Alzheimer's.

Physiologically speaking, the right frontal lobe of the brain controls the non-verbal aspect of human communication, such as the ability to be aware of emotions or to make facial expressions. The right lobe also manages auditory perception, non-verbal communication and the ability to perceive negative emotions. To me, it makes incredible sense—frontal lobe impairments, which are found in both those with Alzheimer's and those with TBI, include motor skill degradation, such as faulty hand/eye coordination; gross motor impairments; decreased ability to concentrate; memory difficulties; emotional disturbances; speech difficulties; and personality/humor changes. Frontal lobe damage can also impair attention span, motivation, social skills, speech, judgment, and organizational capacity.

***

The two stories that follow describe individuals, who, had they been diagnosed properly and been treated accordingly, could have avoided many life challenges. Both cases portray the importance of an environment of nurturing love and harmony and further exemplify that behavior is language.

Linda
The superintendent of a county Board of Developmental Disabilities asked me to attend an emergency meeting for Linda, a young adult who loved Barbie dolls and lived with over a hundred residents at a county developmental center. Linda had a dual diagnosis of severe mental illness and mental retardation and exhibited challenging behaviors. (I believe her diagnosis was incorrect—Linda exhibited signs of mental illness, but mental retardation? No, likely not. In retrospect, I suspect Linda was autistic.)

Linda's behavior and history of severely injuring staff and residents was jeopardizing the Medicaid accreditation of the institution. I asked the interdisciplinary team to describe the behaviors Linda would exhibit before her behavioral outbursts. They indicated that "she would try to run away," so the staff would attempt to stop her. I said that if I had mental illness and heard voices in a setting with more than 100 other people, I would probably run away too! I suggested that they allow me to develop a supported living arrangement where

Linda could live with roommates in their own apartment with a 24-hour staff. The team laughed at me and said, "If a staff of more than 200 can't keep her from running away, how do you propose one staff member can stop her?"

I stated that I believe behavior is language and asked if they had ever considered that her actions were her way of saying that she didn't like it there.

The team was skeptical about my theory and my suggested remedy to the problem; nevertheless, only days after our consultation, Linda severely injured another resident and was taken to University Hospital in Cincinnati, where she was restrained in a padded room and loaded up with the antipsychotic drug Thorazine. I hardly recognized her.

The superintendent then authorized me to do whatever was necessary to resolve Linda's situation.

After persuading, the state to convert her Medicaid funding into supported-living money that would follow her into the community instead of funding a bed in an intermediate care facility (ICF). I settled Linda in the community and trained the staff to provide an empowering environment where she had choices. Linda rarely exhibited the behaviors that led to her hospitalization. Unfortunately, when her home was taken over by another agency that didn't maintain the harmonious and empowering interactions I advocated, Linda's behaviors returned.

***

Far too often, whether in homes where adults with developmental disabilities or in facilities where seniors with dementia reside, employees treat residents like children and assume an authoritarian role. The response of staff is often based on whether residents or clients are compliant ("being good"). My experience and perspective is that people who resort to authoritarian behavior lack a genuine belief in themselves and harbor a basic mistrust and even fear of life and feel they have to be in full control at all times. Consequently, in caregiving situations, such individuals often don't allow the people in their care to make empowering choices or to become self-reliant.

***

Connie
When I met Connie, our agency was just beginning to gain recognition for our ability to transform the lives of people with previously

challenging existences. Connie was 18 and had severe self-inflicted damage to her eyes and significant hearing impairment from repeated, chronic head banging.

Connie spent most of her day in an adjustable bed, restrained at the wrists and ankles to prevent her from injuring herself further.

Before Connie was eleven years old, she had her sight and hearing, went to school, and was known as a very creative and giving person. According to a school psychologist, Connie lost her sight shortly before turning 12 because of her self-destructive behavior and was never the same. Her mother shared that Connie was shuffled back and forth among the children's hospital to schools for the blind, mental health agencies, and developmental disabilities programs throughout her school years.

Because of her self-destructive behavior, Connie spent the few years before I met her restrained much of the time. I knew with every fiber of my being that a gentle person with enduring patience and a lot of love could help Connie take her life back. In selecting a qualified caregiver for Connie, we required someone who would commit to our agency's philosophies and methods of fostering a safe, positive, nurturing environment.

We were truly blessed when we hired a close neighbor who knew Connie and her family. I give this employee much of the credit for Connie's spectacular success. Another element of my strategy for Connie was for her and the program director—an employee of my agency—to bond. I suggested speaking and singing to her in a soft, calm voice; although we did not know how much she would hear or see, I knew from previous experience that many blind and deaf people can see some light, shapes, and shadows and can hear certain sounds.

I also recommended that they softly massage Connie's forehead, arms, and legs and to keep looking at her body language to determine her comfort level. The gentle touch along with softly spoken words and song created a loving and peaceful atmosphere which was very soothing for Connie's physical being and for her entire psyche, including her mental and emotional self.

In other words, Connie felt safe with her new friends and began to feel more comfortable with her world.

I worked with Connie in 1990 before I learned about the sensory issues those with autism face. At that time, I did not believe Connie was autistic, although in retrospect, I believe she was born with a severe case of Asperger's Syndrome that was compounded and complicated by various environmental issues and perhaps some mental health issues. (In the 1970s, '80s, and '90s, many individuals with Asperger's were misdiagnosed as emotionally or mentally ill, ADHD, or just "bad kids.")

After a week of establishing the gentle rapport with Connie, the staff began removing her restraints—first the right hand and then both arms and hands the following day. They continued removing her restraints periodically for several weeks, but Connie's new freedom was often met with attempts of self-abuse.

During this period of nurturing, trust-building, and soothing Connie's frustrations, the staff discovered Connie's passion: before her almost fatal self-abuse, Connie's sisters and mother had taught her to knit and crochet. It was a Herculean challenge for the staff allowing her to use these tools without further damaging her eyes, but if you could have seen the pleasure and tranquility expressed on Connie's face when she was knitting, you would know why we were willing to take the risk. Consequently, I believe allowing Connie to engage in this fulfilling activity was one of the major ingredients of our treatment plan and was a catalyst in her rehabilitation.

After Connie's first month in the new environment, her care team had established a trusting, loving, bond with her, and Connie gradually required less time in arm restraints. The next step was to gradually remove her leg restraints and escort her around the house. As with the process of freeing her from her arm restraints, giving Connie access to the house resulted in similar challenges and periodic behavioral episodes.

At this time, I began to wonder whether Connie's head banging and face and eye striking could be an indication of physical pain or discomfort. Was she simply responding to her discomfort with self-abuse? I considered the possibility that severe headaches or even earaches could be causing her discomfort and prompting her to hurt herself. Here again was an illustration that behavior is language! Like many people with autism and Alzheimer's, could Connie's non-verbal behaviors be communicating her feelings about her body, mind, and environment?

With spring approaching, we determined that it was time for Connie to re-enter the outside world. Her evolution of rehabilitation was so rewarding for the entire team! Like a mother bird pushing her baby out of the nest, we were all almost as anxious as Connie was. Connie, although apprehensive, displayed mostly enthusiasm for her new found freedom. Several months and years passed, and Connie progressed wonderfully. She attended a local school for the blind and learned sign language. Eventually we were able to move Connie into her own home with shift staff to assist her. She did experience several setbacks over the years, but in most cases—if not all—these setbacks were related to the behavior or attitudes of aggressive or controlling residential or day program staff.

The last I heard, Connie was involved in an entrepreneurial program to help her make, promote and sell her beautiful tapestries.

***

I believe that everyone has the ability to shine once given the chance. No matter how disabled or different, everyone has a gift, talent, or purpose that can make a valuable contribution. As I mentioned previously, I believe that Connie was either born with Asperger's Syndrome or, at the least, had autistic tendencies that clashed with her environmental challenges growing up in a very poor neighborhood with an under-educated mother and without a father. Therefore, I have speculated that Connie had autism, aphasia, OCD, and some form of mental illness in addition to all of her other challenges. Can you imagine a world where you are tactile-defensive with significant aversions to certain sounds, smells, and sudden noises, especially with higher intensities? And then add hearing voices and obsessive tendencies—can you see how these characteristics would be challenging for any person, especially with difficult domestic issues? It is my theory that either Connie's outer world was causing her great physical pain or she literally didn't want to see or hear what was going on in her external world.

***

It has been my understanding through the years that like TBI, those with autism also share abnormalities in the frontal lobes, cerebellum, and limbic system, which makes sense to me considering that the neurological results are similar among TBI, autism, and Alzheimer's primarily in the area of emotions (impulsivity) and motor control.

The aforementioned scenarios are only a few examples of the many people I have observed who were able to transcend their previous dispositions. My experience with persons with TBI and Autism provided me with the skills to not only help redirect my own mother and prevent her from becoming anxious and agitated but was able to train her home health staff to do the same. Furthermore, I was able to assist her nursing home and assisted-living staff and residents in facilitating the most harmonious outcomes.

John Zeisel, in his book, *I'm Still Here,* encourages non-pharmacological treatments as much as possible, using pharmaceutical treatments when necessary. He recommends the following three-step approach:

1. Describe behavior and identify contextual triggers.
2. Adapt the caregiver, physical environment, or medication regimen (the context).
3. Employ lowest possible dosage of pharmacologic treatment to make up the difference if needed.[1]

In summary, behavior is language, so once we have interpreted what the behavior is communicating, we must use empowerment, rapport, and valuing—concepts we discussed in the last chapter.

Attitude is everything, and your actions, reactions, responses, demeanor, mood, and the environment can determine the outcome of the subsequent events and experiences of everyone involved.

---

1   John Zeisel, *I'm Still Here: A New Philosophy of Alzheimer's Care,* (New York, NY: Penguin Group, 2010), p. 47.

CHAPTER 8

Is Anyone In There?

The current medical and scientific conclusion about the causes of Alzheimer's is that it is a progressive degenerative brain disease caused when the neuronal connections between brain cells degenerate and die, causing a decline in memory and neural function. Many other scientists believe an increase in a protein beta-amyloid leads to nerve cell death. Neuroscience tells us the hippocampus is the part of the brain that is responsible for memory forming, organizing and storing. Still other scientists and doctors, including Dr. Peter Whitehouse, whom I mention in Chapter 1, are starting to discover flaws in existing theories of the causes of Alzheimer's and are advancing different theories, for example, that Alzheimer's is more a case of human brain aging caused by a number of factors than it is "a disease."

Here is my personal quandary about conditions of the brain: if memory and consciousness are solely dependent on a physical brain, then can we have any memory—or more importantly consciousness—or any "sense" of identity without a physical body? And what happens to our mind or consciousness when we, and hence our brains, die?

And so my logical mind asks how one can believe in science and still believe in eternal life. Earlier in my life, this question inspired me to explore quantum physics and to ask what comes first—the mind/consciousness or the physical body, including the brain, with the mind and subsequent memories and consciousness following?

What happened to my "former mom"—the one from before the Alzheimer's? Assuming her hippocampus was irrevocably damaged, had she lost her memories and identity forever? Had her memories and personal identity been erased from the hippocampus? And what is happening with autistic individuals when they "zone out" and seem to be elsewhere?

Where do people with Alzheimer's and autism "go" when they seem not to be in reality with us? Are they perhaps in a state much like dreaming? Haven't you ever awakened from a dream and it seemed so real that it was *surreal* (beyond real)? Perhaps in your dream you were a younger version of you—I know that I have dreamt about people I went to elementary school with whom I have not thought of in years. Have you dreamt of people in a vivid dream that you do not know in this life, but who seem so familiar in your dream world? Such dreams are fascinating: it is like watching a home movie from the past. I ask myself if it's possible that such a real-seeming dream state could actually *be real*. And if so, perhaps this same state/place/dream world is where individuals with autism and Alzheimer's "go" as well—except in their waking hours?

For me, such questions culminate in the following, larger questions: "Is the psyche dependent on the physical brain and all of its neurological functions? Or does consciousness (or aspects of consciousness) exist on its own, exclusive of the physical structure of the body/brain?"

Roger Lewin, a British science writer and author of 20 books, published an article in *Science* magazine, "Is Your Brain Really Necessary?" about the studies of an English pediatrics professor, Dr. John Lorber.[1] In the 1970s and early 1980s, Lorber studied the brains of patients with hydrocephalus ("water on the brain"), a build-up of cerebrospinal fluid that causes backup of fluid in the skull. Hydrocephalus usually causes mental and physical damage to the person, and if not treated, generally leads to death.

In his paper, Lewin tells the story of a university student Lorber studied "... who has an IQ of 126, has gained a first-class honors degree in mathematics, and is socially completely normal. Yet the boy has virtually no brain." The student's physician at the university noticed that the young man had a slightly larger-than-normal head, and so referred him to Lorber, simply out of interest. According to Lewin, Lorber recalled that "When we did a brain scan on him, we saw thickness of brain tissue between the ventricles and the cortical surface; there was just a thin layer of mantle measuring a millimeter or so. His cranium is filled mainly with cerebrospinal fluid."

Of Lorber's work, David Bowsher, a professor neurophysiology in Liverpool, England, says that although "Lorber's work doesn't demonstrate that we don't need a brain, it does show that the brain can work in conditions we would have thought were impossible."[2]

So although we have come far in understanding the biological ramifications of the brain, we still have far to go!

Thoughts on the consciousness-brain relationship prompt me to ask questions about my mother's Alzheimer's experience. How can it be that my mother at one point mentally deteriorated to the extent that she did not remember much of anything and often thought I was her brother—but then, after moving from a nursing home into a family home, her once-banished memory started to re-surface? One

---

1   Roger Lewin, "Is Your Brain Really Necessary?" *Science*, December 12, 1980:Vol. 2 10 no. 4475 pp. 1232-1234

2 "Where Is Consciousness? I've Lost It!: Is the Brain Really Necessary?"
    <http://flatrock.org.nz/topics/science/is_the_brain_really_necessary.htm>

would think that once the hippocampus is damaged, those memories are lost forever and would not be retrievable at a later time.

I believe that the more nurturing, loving environment not only renewed her stamina and physical heath, but it improved her attitude and her memory as well. After the move, my mother's overall memory improved, and I was amazed at her ability to remember the early 1940s in specific detail. She started asking about the people with whom she had gone to junior high school, using their first and last names. I had never heard of many of these individuals. Being curious, I went to her former home, went through her old pictures, and discovered an autograph book with the names of most of the people she had asked about. This acute past memories phase lasted for about a month.

One Saturday during this extraordinary month, she literally took us down memory lane by showing us where she lived when she first arrived in Dayton, Ohio. She gave us the actual street address and pointed out who lived where. She got anxious at one point when she wanted us to stop at the home of one of the neighbors of whom she'd been very fond. She got extremely upset at my partner Leslie and me when we told her that we could not stop for a visit because the family had not lived there for 55 years! (I learned later not to argue with her, as there was no convincing her otherwise, and we would go along with her and say things such as, "Hmmm, I don't think they're home, Mom.")

Much of western medicine and science have their foundations in the old Descartes and Newtonian mechanistic models of the universe, which more or less separate the ideas of math, thought, and spirit. Historically, the root of most theories is that we and the rest of the universe have evolved from physical and biological phenomena. Little or no research on spiritual consciousness or free will exists. I believe that the current discussion of quantum physics will inspire a new science where science, metaphysics, and spirituality will merge.

During my informal research into Alzheimer's, I repeatedly heard stories of how loved ones, during their last stages of Alzheimer's, had moments of lucid memory—a brief return to their former personalities. Jonathon Franzen, in his article in the *New Yorker* called *My Father's Brain*, shares the following:

> *Consider what I believe are the last words he ever spoke to me, three months before he died. For a couple of days, I'd been visiting the nursing home for a dutiful 90 minutes and listening to his mutterings about my mother and to his affable speculations about certain tiny objects that he*

persisted in seeing on the sleeves of his sweater and the knees of his pants. He was no different when I dropped by on my last morning, no different when I wheeled him back to his room and told him I was heading out of town. But when he raised his face toward mine and—again, out of nowhere, his voice was clear and strong—he said, "Thank you for coming. I appreciate your taking the time to see me." Set phrases of courtesy? A window on his fundamental self? I seem to have little choice about which version to believe.[3]

So could it be that we have a nonphysical consciousness counterpart (our soul self) including our mind/memories to our cells and entire physical body including the brain? Much like how you are reading this book in the physical (on your eReader or in printed form), but you cannot destroy its original source—like the hard drive on my computer?

Jill Bolte Taylor, a Harvard-trained brain scientist, illustrates her belief that there are silver linings in what most people would perceive as catastrophe. Taylor, at 37 years old, had a stroke that damaged the left side of her brain and forced her to compensate with her intuitive right brain. In the last chapter of her book, *My Stroke of Insight: A Brain Scientist's Personal Journey*, Dr. Taylor exclaims, "I have learned so much from this experience with stroke, that I actually feel fortunate to have taken this journey."[4]

Dr. Taylor does a great job of explaining the different functions of the right versus left hemisphere of the brain. Her stroke experience afforded her the opportunity to actually feel the concept of "simply being." Her writing is full of such exclamations as, "My soul was as big as the universe and frolicked with glee in a boundless sea."[5] "All I could perceive was right here, right now, and it was beautiful!"[6] "Everything in my visual world blended together, and with every pixelatating energy, we all flowed en masse, together as one."[7] And "In the absence of my left hemisphere negative judgment, I perceived myself as perfect, whole, and beautiful just the way I was."[8]

In other words, instead of being stuck in despair, she made peace with what was and discovered an actual gift! Despair would not have

3 Jonathon Franzen, "My Father's Brain," *The New Yorker*, September 10, 2001, p. 80.
4 Jill Bolte Taylor, *My Stroke of Insight: A Brain Scientist's Personal Journey*: (New York: Viking Penguin, 2006) p. 175.
5 Ibid. p. 69
6 Ibid. pp. 68-69
7 Ibid. p. 69-70
8 Ibid. p. 71

undone that long road to recovery, but a more positive attitude and self-determination would and did make it less burdensome

You will understand the point I am making if you believe in near-death experiences (NDEs) and have read about someone who lay dying and, although unconscious, leaves their body but maintains their identity and memories. There has to be a non-physical, spiritual aspect to human beings, whether you call it spirit, soul, or oversoul! Out of all the NDE books I have read, the most convincing was *Dying to Be Me*, by Anita Moorjani.

Moorjani shares her horrific four-year cancer battle and how the malignant cells began to shut down her organs. In my opinion, Moorjani's journey from end-stage lymphoma, to a period of lucid unconsciousness, to awakening completely healthy and healed not only exemplifies the classic near-death experience, but attests to the power of our mind-spirit-body connection to heal us of even the most dreadful diseases or accidents.

How would the medical community explain the following story from my own father's passing? During his last hours of life, we were told that he could never regain consciousness because his vital organs were shutting down. Right before his death, he turned his head slightly toward my mom and me, and using two fingers of his right hand, made motions of a pair of scissors on his beard. We knew instantly what his last request was to be clean shaven for the funeral visitation.

I believe that skepticism can be healthy, but I also believe that it is healthy to be skeptical about the theory that NDEs are merely biological occurrences—for example, oxygen deprivation to the brain—that cause one to see or hear things that appear to be supernatural. In my opinion, if the NDE phenomenon were not credible, would so many respected professionals jeopardize their reputations by sharing their own and their patients' NDE stories?

Take, for instance, the stories of Mary Neal, M.D. and Eben Alexander, M.D., both of whom have written books recounting their near-death experiences. Dr. Neal, an orthopedic surgeon, has written a book called *To Heaven and Back*, which tells her remarkable story about drowning in a Kayak accident and being encouraged by her angels to return to her body. Dr. Alexander's book, *Proof of Heaven*, tells his story of life-threatening bacterial meningitis and his journey to the afterlife and back.

Now let us return to the subject of those with Alzheimer's and autism. I ponder the experiences of many people with these conditions—which most people dismiss as hallucinations, delusions, or the effects of brain disorders. The longer I live, the more I believe that many of these people are tapping into other dimensions. Ninety percent of the people we interviewed for this book tell stories of their loved ones with dementia seeing or hearing people, animals, or things that others could not perceive.

My friend Vickie Rogers told me this story about her mother-in-law, who had Alzheimer's:

> *She was a wonderful, high-spirited, loving lady who always donated her time to sing at nursing homes. Before she died, she would only stare off into space like nobody was home inside. Nevertheless, she suddenly would look out the window and say, "See him? He is over there." Or she would see her mom and call out to her deceased husband. One thing I noticed—although she couldn't talk intelligently—whenever I would start singing a song, she would come to life and sing the song in perfect pitch! We would bring her a card sometimes, and she would be able to read it.*

Vickie also shared that her own mother, while on her deathbed, saw visions of people who had died and that she saw her brother who had died three weeks before—about whose death the doctor had recommended keeping a secret so as not to upset her!

My own mother would often see children playing out in the yard or at the park and would get so frustrated when we could not see them. When my sister tried to convince her that there's no way she could have seen our dad or her dad, my mother would shout out, "But I just saw him yesterday!" To reduce her frustration level, as I mentioned previously, we started to go along with her.

Some quantum physicists believe that all time is simultaneous and that there are many versions of reality—so-called parallel universes. So let us speculate and say that if there is any validity or possibility to this theory, could mom have been merely tapping into different periods of her life or seeing alternate timelines?

Could those Leonardo Da Vinci drawings of the tank, helicopter, and other "futuristic" inventions not be necessarily "visionary," but rather be the result of Da Vinci actually tapping into a 21st century reality that existed simultaneous to his own 15th century? Could that explain my mother's vivid memories of the early 1940s? Could it be that for people like my mom or people seeing their life pass before them that existence is like a DVD, and they are simply jumping among various tracks?

My friend who has Asperger's, Nancy, says on her website, "Autistic individuals live in a world of their own due to inherited genes that affect the frontal lobe (cerebrum and limbic system) of the brain. This is one of the theories currently being researched to discover the cause of this mysterious disorder, and it is the theory that I believe will one day unlock the door to this secret world."

Speaking of this "secret world," let's consider the so-called hallucinations that people with autism experience: I have observed many with autism who carry on one or more conversations with several imaginary characters, sometimes in different voices. The most fascinating of all of my observations was from my time as a manager of a group home. One older resident, who rarely talked around others, stuttered in fragmented sentences. I discovered that when he was alone, however, he would carry on intellectual conversations with two or sometimes three imaginary people. I believe his primary character—Dr. Brown—was supposed to be a professor who would carry on sophisticated intellectual conversations with several others. The most fascinating aspect of this example to me is that not only was this individual autistic, but he was also labeled profoundly mentally retarded. Before moving to the group home, he lived in a state institution in Ohio called Orient, where I am sure he never shared that part of himself with others and especially not with any psychologist.

Therefore, I am beginning to believe in a common association and relationship among those with autism and Alzheimer's with their biological brain and their mental, spiritual, consciousness of the psyche.

If you are like me, you will end this chapter (and probably this book) with more questions than answers. In researching this book, I have come to believe that this phenomenon is not merely a subject from the twilight zone, the paranormal, or science fiction, and is finally being studied as a valid scientific phenomenon in the traditional medical and psychology communities.

I do not believe in accidents or coincidence. Case in point: as I was about to end this chapter, I turned on National Public Radio to hear Terry Gross on her show *Fresh Air*, and she was interviewing a Dr. Sam Parnia, a critical care doctor and director of resuscitation research at the Stony Brook University School of Medicine in Stony Brook, New York. He was discussing his new book, *Erasing Death: The Science that is Rewriting the Boundaries Between Life and Death*.

According to Dr. Parnia, post-death phenomena and experiences have primarily been explored and debated by philosophers and clergy. Now, with the advent of modern sophisticated technology, physicians are able to biologically keep a body alive as more and more consciousness returns to the body. Consequently, such post-death phenomena are increasingly being studied and researched by neuroscientists, psychiatrists and psychologists, and neurologists.

On the *Fresh Air* show, *"Erasing Death" Explores the Science of Resuscitation*, Dr. Parnia says the following about what he calls "after death" experiences:

> *Now, what we study is not people who are near death. We study people who have objectively died. These people have been dead for tens, sometimes hours—tens of minutes and sometimes hours of time. And therefore, what we've understood is that the experience that these people have of going beyond the threshold of death, entering the period after death for the first few minutes, tens of minutes or hours of time, provides us with an indication of what we're all likely to experience when we go through death.*[9]

Dr. Parnia stated that he has studied research from all over the world and people from various races, cultures, religions, and even atheists who claimed to have similar after-death experiences and memories. These shared experiences include similar stories of our out-of-body experiences, tunnels, bright light, luminous divine beings, and the most joyful, peaceful feelings ever experienced.

Recent studies and common reports from scientific studies verifying thousands of incidents of out-of-body episodes document patients having total recall of what was happening in the emergency or operating room during a time the brain was clinically dead. Memories include vivid conversations between medical staff and knowledge of special signs placed on the ceilings of the treatment room.

In an early chapter, my co-author Nancy Reder writes that it has been discussed in scientific circles that Leonardo Da Vinci had Asperger's. Dr. Parnia, in the *Fresh Air* interview, talks about a painting by another artist from the 15th century, Hieronymus Bosch:

> *There's a very interesting painting by Hieronymus Bosch from the 15th century where he's actually painted what looks like a classical near-death experience, but in reality people didn't know about near-death experiences at that time, and it certainly isn't what classical Christianity would have taught of what people would have experienced when they've died.*[10]

---

9   "'Erasing Death' Explores the Science of Resuscitation." Fresh Air. National Public Radio. 20 February 2013. Web. Transcript.
10 Ibid.

Could it be that Bosch, like Da Vinci, was gifted with Asperger's?

Later, a day after hearing the NPR interview, I received a phone call from a gentleman from California named Joe, who became one of the contributors to this book, who wanted to know more about our book research. Joe is on the eighth year of his Alzheimer's diagnosis and said he agrees with my theory that for many with Alzheimer's, it is God's way of soothing the death transition. He stated that he was fearful of the death process, but after several years living with Alzheimer's, he has no fear of the initial termination neither of life nor of the afterlife. He also shared in our phone conversation that he became less uptight and more calm and peaceful with himself and others after he had Alzheimer's for a while.

In his story, called *Caught Between Realities*, Joe makes reference to a popular quote: "We are spiritual beings having a physical experience instead of physical beings having a spiritual experience." I believe it's entirely possible that those people with Autism and Alzheimer's, those who have had near-death experiences, and those in coma who can recall exact conversations and events that occurred around them—and even ourselves during our dreams—may be tapping into other dimensions where the spiritual aspect of who we are is all the more real.

Albert Einstein and Thomas Edison both claimed that many of their insights came in dreams. So could those people with Alzheimer's like my mom or those who die shortly after a coma actually just be acclimating—through their condition—to the eternal afterlife that we will all one day experience? I myself believe that when we make that spiritual trip, we will take the fond memories, wisdom, and lessons we gleaned from our journey on earth with us.

Perhaps this is the only way for us to discover some of the answers to the perplexing questions this book asks?

Living In Joy: The Role of Chronic Stress

After interviewing hundreds of people (families and professionals), conducting countless of hours of research, and reading at least 50 books, I have no absolute opinion on the causes of autism or Alzheimer's disease.

However, I definitely feel that long-term chronic stress, a lifetime of emotional instability, and resisting life all play a major role in damaging the immune system, consequently perhaps causing the form of dementia called Alzheimer's disease.

I have always heard that autism is a genetic disorder in neural development provoked by environmental factors. Recently, after reading the book *Autism* by Dr. Robert Melillo, I believe that epigenetics and stress on the mother, especially during pregnancy, contribute to the development of autism. According to Webster's dictionary, epigenetics is the theory that the embryo, influenced by its internal and external environment, develops progressively by stages, forming structures that were not originally present in the egg. If I understand correctly, the author is saying that the infant's brain formation has been compromised by various environmental factors that have turned off key genes. Consequently, if true, future parents are not victims of their genetics, but can have more control on the outcome of the child's anatomy. Furthermore, Dr. Melillo gives future parents hope with the progress science is making with neuroplasticity, which refers to an adaptable brain at any age making new neurons and rewiring the brain, creating a new neural pathways.

Dr. Joe Dispenza has written a book that explains to readers "how to lose your mind and create a new one." In his book *Breaking the Habit of Being Yourself*, Dr. Dispenza starts with the premise (to which I also subscribe) that if our thoughts can make us sick, they can makes us well too! He provides excellent illustrations of how our thoughts and emotions regulate our glandular and neurological chemistry and systems. Moreover, he provides methods and techniques for how to consciously transform and control the biochemical effects of our thoughts, feelings, and expectations that can determine whether we have health or illness.

Dr. Bruce Lipton, author of *Biology of Belief*, and Dr. Dispenza write and lecture on neuroplasticity and how changing our beliefs can literally not only rewire the brain, but also control and determine genetic propensities. Daniel Amen M.D., author of *Change Your Brain, Change Your Life*, writes the following in his foreword of Dr. Dispenza's book: "Disease like Alzheimer's actually starts in the brain decades before people have any symptoms."[1] I also lecture and teach the impact of beliefs and until *Gifts* my most popular book was *Beliefology: Raise Your Consciousness to Wealth Health & Happiness*.

In his book, *Autism*, Dr. Melillo says:

Where there is chronic stress, there is usually inflammation, and where there are both, there most likely is a brain imbalance. Inflammatory chronic illness and autoimmune disease are part and parcel of an immune system out of balance.[2]

I have read in other sources that high levels of the so-called stress hormone, cortisol, are present in children with autism.

Dr. Melillo continues by stating:

Immune problems are common in both autistic children and their mothers. I do not believe it is a coincidence when we discover that a woman with a right brain deficit, a chronically elevated stress response, and an overactive immune system ends up with a child who has autism.[3]

Marx points out in an[4] article about the role the immune system plays on the process of the development of Alzheimer's that "Alzheimer's disease is a good example how an immune response may lead to tissue destruction and neuronal loss instead of maintaining the integrity of the body."

The book that most influenced my opinion regarding the significant role of stress and emotional repression is *When the Body Says No* by Dr. Gabor Mate. Dr. Mate explores the stress-disease connections after he and his family were introduced to the horrific stress of

---

1   Dispenza, Joe, *Breaking the Habit of Being Yourself: How to Lose Your Mind and Create a New One* (Carlsbad, CA: Hay House, Inc., 2012), p.xii

2   Ibid., p. 208

3   Ibid., p. 208-209

4   F. Marx, 'Mechanisms of immune regulations in Alzheimer's disease: a viewpoint" arch Immunol Ther Exp al (warsz) 1999, 47(4) 205-9

surviving Nazi genocide. As an infant, Dr. Gabor was separated from his father, and he and his mother nearly starved while held captive in Budapest under Nazi occupation. His maternal grandparents were killed in Auschwitz when he was five months old. Clearly, this book makes a persuasive argument about the relationship between stress and emotional competence in all disease. Consider the authors questions:

> Could early life experiences, emotional repression and lifelong stress predispose to Alzheimer's? Scientific research indicates so, as does a close look at the lives of people with Alzheimer's—whether common folk or the famous like Swift or the former U.S. president Ronald Regan. [5]

In this book, which I highly recommend, the doctor claims as follows:

> One of the first structures to deteriorate in Alzheimer's is the hippocampus, a center of grey matter in the temporal lobe of the brain, located to either side next to the ears. The hippocampus is active in memory formations and has an important function in stress regulation. It is well known that chronically high levels of the stress hormone cortisol can shrink the hippocampus.[6]

My friend Joe, who has Alzheimer's and has contributed his story to this book, sent me a link to a Weblog ("blog") site called RavenstarHealingRooms Blog that includes a relevant quote by Deb Shapiro under the topic "Understanding the emotional/spiritual aspects of Alzheimer's disease."

In Alzheimer's ...

> ... there is a withdrawal of the life-giving emotional input, resulting in deep mental trauma. This trauma may be an intense fear of what lies ahead in old age and death, so much so that there is a reversion to childlike behavior and a shutting down of present-day awareness as a way of ignoring the future. This state has also been described as a preparation time, a period when we can play out our

---

5   Maté, Gabor, *When the Body Says No: Exploring the Stress-Disease Connection* (Hoboken, NJ: John Wiley & Sons, Inc, 2003), p.158
6   Ibid.

fears and fantasies while living in a semi-alive state, a state that can even border on keen awareness and understanding. Then when death comes, it is not so fraught with the terror of letting go. [7]

Prevention and Acting as if You are Young!

Dr. Peter Whitehouse, a practicing geriatric neurologist and one of the best-known Alzheimer's experts in the world, provides a provocative and unique perspective on dementia. His wonderful book, *The Myths of Alzheimer's*, reduces some of the fear surrounding Alzheimer's and emphasizes the need to focus on current and future needs of people with Alzheimer's and their families instead of putting disproportionate amounts of resources on possible cures.

Says Dr. Whitehouse about his book: "This book ultimately seeks to nurture the unfolding of your story. It is about overcoming your fear of Alzheimer's disease by gaining knowledge about brain aging and learning to reframe a narrative for yourselves that will promote quality of life, cognitive vitality, and a sense of purpose and community as you age."[8]

During our research of all the books on Alzheimer's written by physicians, I found Dr. Whitehouse the best. Not only did it help me reframe my perspective of Alzheimer's, but I also felt relieved by his empowering, practical information on how to age gracefully.

Changing the way we view things can change your life, and the story that you wish to live by as you age as a human being is very much in your power to choose. If we reframe the way we think, speak, and act toward our aging brains and integrate new language, new psychosocial understandings, beliefs, attitudes, prevention measures, and treatment options into our biomedical paradigm of AD, we can reimagine the story of Alzheimer's disease and describe brain aging in a way that brings quality to people's latter years rather than adding distress and fear and that better helps our society prepare for a challenging future.[9]

So the common theme that I gleaned from those books that resonated with me was that perhaps we may reduce or eliminate the probability of getting Alzheimer's or other forms of dementia by reducing our anxiety and reducing the stress that enhances certain hormones that

---

7   Shapiro, Deb, <ravenstarshealingroom.wordpress.com/?s=alzheimer's>
8   Whitehouse, Peter, *The Myths of Alzheimer's* (New York, NY: St. Martin's Press, 2008), p. 45.
9   Ibid., p. 44

may damage the hippocampus and other parts of the nervous system effecting memory.

In *The Myths of Alzheimer's*, Dr. Whitehouse provides an eclectic array of preventative measures to promote healthy memories, mind, and body, including alternative and traditional medicine, nutrition, exercise, life style changes, and stress reduction strategies. This book and John Zeisel's book, *I'm Still Here*, provide new and innovative approaches and treatments for those who already have Alzheimer's or autism.

One of the many "gifts" I received from my mom's experience was the reality check that I was almost 60 and that I did not want to be frail, sick, and especially not a nursing home resident. I have always been more of a mental person and have not been very physically active. I looked around and saw people at the nursing home younger than myself. Over weight with sleep apnea, this wake-up call also convinced me to lose weight. The "great recession" of recent years forced me out of full-time consulting and workshop presenting into taking a job and establishing a wellness and fitness program for people with developmental disabilities.

My new-found quest for enhanced health and wellness inspired the name "Ability to Thrive," which my employer agreed to. We teach best what we need to learn.

Finally, as I conclude with you this journey of discovering the hidden gifts in Autism and Alzheimer's, I am aware that another gift my experiences have given me is my awareness of the benefits of thinking and acting young! Have you noticed how infants, children, teenagers, and young adults in their 20s are, as a rule, more enthusiastic, optimistic, vital, lively, happy, joyful, and active than us old fogies?

It is my observation, in general, the older people get, the more rigid, grumpy, critical, controlling, and pessimistic they get, not to mention less active, more negative, fearful, and anxious. I am not saying everyone—I know personally and have heard about people in their 80s and 90s (and even centurions) who take risks and are active, healthy, flexible, confident, happy, and joyful—and who never complain or worry.

Guess what? These individuals are often sharp minded, flexible, healthy in their bodies, spirits, and minds! Yes, they may have some arthritis or forget their keys more than the younger ones, but even with these less serious pains, they don't complain, but rather appreciate what they do have, and what others do and are, and live life to the fullest.

And I know you may be saying that younger people have their issues as well!

Dr. Robert Melillo has a final note in his Autism book entitled getting back our "right mind." He discusses the balance that nature created between the two sides of the brain. He claims that sensory overload with technology and environmental toxins—as well as society's left brain-dominating tendencies along with genetic predisposition—are causing a shift towards left-brain dominance. Our society emphasizes and indoctrinates us to left-brain *doing* versus the importance of the right-brain *being*!

In a previous chapter I shared how Dr. Jill Bolte Taylor's experience with a stroke gave her insights such as peace was only a thought away when she learned to quiet her pre-stroke dominating mind.

She says, "Based upon my experience with losing my left mind, I whole-heartedly believe that the feeling of deep inner peace is neurologically circuitry located in our right brain."[10]

Although there has been much debate about right vs. left brain function, most scientists would agree there are dominant characteristics to each hemisphere, as follows:

LEFT BRAIN	RIGHT BRAIN
Masculine	Feminine
Yang	Yin
More thinking	More feeling
Ego dominance	Inner, authentic self
Analytical, judging, critical	Diplomatic and perceptive
Logical/linear, calculating	Creative, expressive, artistic
(Head) logical	(Heart) intuitive
Practical	Adventurous
Security-minded	Open-minded
Detail-oriented	Big picture-oriented
Simple, fact-based, evidence-based	Allow things to happen
Verbal language	Body language
Make things happen	Perceptive of others' intentions & feelings

Before I conclude this chapter, I would like to share the final note excerpt from Dr. Melillos book, *Autism*.:

---

10   Jill Bolte Taylor, *My Stroke of Insight: A Brain Scientist's Personal Journey*: (New York: Viking Penguin, 2006), p. 159.

I believe that this epidemic of autism and other similar neurological disorders is a product of our environment, and that it is a powerful wake-up call to all of us telling us that we need to care more for our planet and one another. We need to explore the world around us and reconnect, person to person. We need to re-establish a balance between good old-fashioned ideals, thoughts, and behaviors with the convenience of modern technology and information. In short, we need to get back in balance.[11]

So how can we reduce our stress resistance to life's events and became more honest and open in expressing our authentic powerful selves to optimum wellness? How can we become more centered and more calm and peaceful, thereby balancing our serotonin and cortisol levels? It should not take Alzheimer's or a stroke to teach us how to empower and savor the moment. Let us spend less time with television, cell phones, and other gadgets and get back to enjoying and vibrating with nature. Become one with the running brook, sunrise, sunset, blades of grass, trees, and leaves, flowers and their petals. Play Pollyanna's glad game and find something to be glad for. Don't be sad or mad ... "be glad!"

No matter what circumstance you find yourself in, search for positive aspects in your life and think about your favorite things and memories. When challenged, don't give your power away; become inner directed! You create what you concentrate on, so when you focus on what you appreciate and are grateful for with positive expectancy, then it is almost impossible to feel mad, sad, or in despair. My spiritual teachers taught me that your power is in this now moment, and if you are centered on your spiritual point of power, you will discover your moment point of peace. As a longtime life coach, I have discovered for myself and countless others that the more I live from the power and peace of my spiritual Self connecting with my higher connection of my God source, the more I attract only the best events, experiences, and circumstances.

I'm a strong believer in positive affirmations, and one of my favorites is "Everything always works out for me!" My other favorite happens to be the title of my spiritual partner's first book: *Trust and Allow the Process of Life, In-Joy!*

Worry and judge less. I wish I could regain the energy I wasted on things that never happened.

---

11   Robert Melillo, *Autism*, (New York, NY: Penguin Group, 2012), p. 298.

Finally, let the enthusiasm, curiosity, joy-filled, wonder-filled, energetic, optimistic inner child out to play and have some FUN and excitement!

Feel young, act young, be young!

Stop giving your life away by caring what other people think about you. Love, accept, and embrace yourself and others unconditionally. Don't waste any more time. Live and savor every day and year like it is your last because time, as well as your life, goes much to fast!

Keep love and joy and hope alive!

Stories of the Spectrum

In this chapter the families of persons with disabilities share their stories. Minimal editing has been done in order to preserve authenticity.

Super Hero—Jake
By Jenn Lynn

We are proud parents of a gorgeous "Super Hero" named Jake. *Labor of the heart* is what we call the adoption of our son. *Labor of love* is what we do every day.

This child, Jake, not only made our family, but he re-created our world by showing us what it's like to live in his.

When we received our son, he was almost three weeks old. His first pediatrician reports superb health, big for his age, very alert and aware. An entire church prayed over him before he and the foster family parted, our hearts were filled with joy and imaginations were full of hope.

We were told by the adoption agency that the biological mother had ADHD and a seizure disorder, which meant anti-seizure meds. We were NOT told about the bipolar disorder, which meant two more anti-psychotics throughout the entire pregnancy. Again we wait, to see how our new baby would develop. Dreams building upon dreams. Love deepening.

Since my husband and I are both the younger kids in our families, we didn't have much experience with newborns and were flying blind in this baby business. Jake was heavy, never stopped moving, and holding him was difficult as he didn't "cling" or "clutch" around the hip as most babies did. I remember my muscles straining and my back spasms clenching as he grew so quickly. Some relatives wondered, but no one spoke a word.

Jake did the army crawl until nine months ... which is when he started running and never stopped. At 14 months, we would log actual running miles with him. He would push a toy, a four-wheeled inch worm, around the neighborhood with glee. The motion was endless, the neighbors would question. I would run behind him for miles a day. (Later we discovered this is calming for his body)

Doctor after doctor was impressed with his physical strength, alertness and agility. We enrolled in two-year-old private preschool and the bells and whistles sounded. After watching our child stand in the corner all morning away from peers, stare at the ceiling fans, pound on a nail/hammer board, chew his fingernails down to the quick, avoid interaction with other children, the staff quickly scheduled our first parent-teacher conference.

Nerves were raw as the teacher and assistant entered the room and handed me a box of tissues. While they are not qualified to diagnose anything, one teacher mentioned that some OT could really help him, as well as getting an evaluation from the county school system. We knew he was different but the thought of autism never crossed our minds. Hyper? Yes.

The Autism Spectrum Disorder diagnosis at nearly three years old broke our hearts, stirred our souls and launched us into action. Intensive needs preschool prep class at the public school started in the mornings when he was three and I copied what they did at home in the afternoons. We were starving for information on how to help our child, so teachers taught us along the way by sending projects home and helping us set up home-school. Intervention was immediate and exhausting, but our bodies ached with a need to help our child to cope and survive in this very confusing and stimulating world.

So many children are delayed treatment because parents aren't ready to accept a diagnosis. One professional pointed out that since Jake was adopted we were fortunate to be able to skip the common "guilt/denial" phase and move right on the mourning, then to action. We cried, yelled, and voiced our anger about his biology while watching him struggle with his hypersensitive system and lagging social skills. Then realized there was no time to waste!

Teachers' were impressed with our determination and dedication. Jake's progress was steady as friends fell away and questions mounted: What will the future hold? What else should we be doing? How can we help him? How can we take the pain away? Our worlds changed as our focused zoned in on success for Jake.

As we devoured books, met with doctors and picked teachers brains, I developed such a respect for our child. Even though his interpretation of life was a violation of his senses, he spoke, forced himself to look people in the eye and fought through the challenges daily living presented. Our love and admiration grew even deeper once we realized just what it takes for him to get through a day.

Early on we decided to never make autism a negative. We have always told Jake he has super powers. He actually does if you think about it. He hears things we don't hear. Sees things we don't notice and smells scents with the acuteness of a hound dog. His ability to sense changes in mood, feeling or energy is amazing. I tell people he knows I'm mad before I even know I'm mad. We've explained to him that his brain works super-fast and we take special medicine to help him slow down and understand. We've taught him that not everyone's brain is so quick so he's doubly blessed.

Soon after diagnosis, we knew we needed to enter his world and adjust ours in order to find success for our super hero. Calendars, schedules and timers still adorn our walls, upstairs and down. Our days start and end with a speed walk around the neighborhood and trampoline/bike time. Any and all changes are prepped and planned until they are predictable. All in the name of keeping Jake comfortable and keeping the peace.

His meltdowns are intense, emotional and physical. Rage strength is real and scary especially now that Jake is big. Keeping Jake regulated, calm and cool is a challenge and unfortunately not achieved without medication. The slippery slope of prescriptions started in kindergarten and we're still slaloming through new scripts. Our lives have morphed from doting parents full of hope to being pharmacologists, psychologists, behaviorists.

Since placement in private school, Jake has gained the tools to express his frustrations and emotions. He has taught us as parents how important it is to qualify and quantify our own emotions. We have learned to say when we are feeling mad, cry when we're feeling sad and talk even when we just want to be alone. We all take Time Outs and Curb Time when we've had enough.

Many people say spectrum kids can't experience compassion, empathy or real unconditional love. That is just not the case. We don't go a day without Jake telling us how much he loves us (completely unprompted) and he feels sad for the less fortunate. True, children are not born with these abilities, they need to be taught and modeled by the parents

Autism has actually brought our family closer, a bond we will need as we mature and grow old. The behavior management/life skills we've incorporated into our household are applied across the board; perspective, compassion and understanding are needed with friends, in the workplace and with aging relatives.

ASD life is an exhausting and endless journey where you need to hunt for the highlights: holding a pencil, cleaning up in the bathroom, using sign language to request something are all reasons to celebrate. Find a support system; it may not be your family; many times its other parents travelling the same road as you.

These kids are amazing gifts and doubly blessed. Don't ever give up hope on your spectrum child. If you do, they have no one else. See your child for the blessing that he/she is and this is your chance to grow and educate the world. Education and awareness leads to ACCEPTANCE!

The Greatest Teacher In My Life: My Daughter
By Cheryl Anne

My greatest blessing arrived after years of prayers, medical procedures, and a very long and painful labor. It was the day I met my daughter for the first time. She was delivered by Caesarean section, so she was placed against my cheek only briefly, before being rushed off to an adjacent room. It took only that split-second for me to realize I would give my life for that tiny beautiful baby; I knew my life was forever changed.

I had no inkling that my daughter and I were about to embark on the most difficult journey of our lives. I couldn't have known then that my perfect child would begin to exhibit signs that something was terribly wrong. Only a few days after our arrival home, she began to cry inconsolably, for hours. She wouldn't nurse and had difficulty holding down any type of formula. She would writhe as if in the most extreme pain for hours until exhausting herself into brief periods of sleep.

The pediatrician explained it was most likely colic, and that it would pass. It didn't. When she was a toddler she began to bang her head on the tile floor, and scream when anyone moved anything in the house. She spoke a few simple words, but most often repeated the end or beginning of a word she heard someone else say. She hated bright light, especially the sunlight. I took her to the beach (my favorite place) she cried when her toes or fingers touched the sand. The sound of a baby crying seemed to torture her, and when my friends brought their toddlers to visit, she cried when any of her toys were touched.

What was happening to my child? I began obsessively reading and asking advice of family members. Didn't they see what I was seeing? Could it be me? The answers and comments were "She is smart and will outgrow it" and "You are looking for something that is not there, all new parents struggle."

After many years of searching for answers, undergoing numerous assessments, misdiagnoses and countless visits to specialists, she would eventually be diagnosed with an Autism Spectrum Disorder (ASD). At the time, I had little idea what that meant. All I knew of autism was that it seemed these children were forever locked into a world of their own, never emerging. Could it be that my child, this little person whom I had so many hopes and dreams for, would never live a life filled with everything I wished for her? I didn't cry when I heard my daughter's final diagnosis. I figured I had cried so much on the path to finding an answer, I ran out of tears. I became numb; I think it was a defense mechanism to protect me from the frequent complaints regarding my daughter's behavior, and the many people who looked at me as though I was a bad parent for allowing my daughter to act out in public. None of this mattered, because no one beat me up more than I beat myself up. The guilt phase had set in with a vengeance.

At the end of second grade, my daughter's speech language pathologist said "She is doing really well and has greatly improved in some of her weakest areas." Those words broke my dry spell. I cried again for the first time in years and my tears of joy were mirrored in the eyes of the others who attended the meeting that day.

I will never forget this day, because it was the day I finally heard someone say something positive about my daughter. Instead of dwelling on the negative, this lovely person (whom I call an angel) helped me change my mindset. She gave me hope and the understanding that I needed to focus on my daughter's gifts. Instead of concentrating on "the big picture," I began to enjoy the small accomplishments my daughter made.

I walked a few inches taller that day, and began to enjoy and accept my daughter for who she was and is. She is the gift I had prayed for. I stopped feeling sorry for myself and for my daughter and decided to model a positive attitude for her, along with the hope of what she could do and would one day become. I was her mother, advocate, and friend. I allowed her to be my teacher because I entered her world, instead of expecting her to fit into mine.

It is difficult to find the words to describe the gifts my daughter has bestowed upon me. Though it was, and continues to be a difficult road for her, she has never complained. I have had to push her hard sometimes to get her to reach her full potential; yet she never held it against me.

While she was in elementary school, the class was asked to write about their "hero." Parents were invited to the classroom to hear the assignments read aloud. Most of the children chose athletes, movie stars, singers and popular bands. Imagine my reaction when I heard my daughter read her essay, naming me as her hero. Again the tears began to flow, and again my tears were mirrored in the eyes of many of the listeners. My daughter is an adult now, but I still keep this essay close by. No matter how many times I read it, I still feel the same gratitude as if I were reading it for the first time. Her essay started "My hero is not famous but she is very close to my heart, she is my mom who dedicated her whole life to helping me." As long as I live, I cannot imagine hearing more beautiful words.

I have learned countless lessons from my daughter, my hero. I know I would not have learned these lessons any other way. I learned the things that I once thought were important are not. She has taught me that life is about struggles and growth, and that knowing one's true self comes out of these struggles. She has shown me the meaning of never giving up and not letting what anyone says about you, force you to quit. She sees the true beauty in people, not in how they look; rather she sees only their genuineness and their inner beauty. She has shown me how to read a person's heart.

I changed careers when my daughter entered middle school. I loved volunteering to meet with other parents who needed guidance, and working directly with children who have ASD. It was so rewarding I decided to return to college to acquire a degree that would allow me to help other families on their personal journeys through ASD, in a more involved way. In my Master's application essay, I wrote that I wanted to obtain my degree so that I could help other children with ASD and their families so that no one had to walk the path alone, as I did. I never want anyone to take this journey without hope, nor to focus on the negative and not see the gifts and strengths of their beautiful children.

Today, I am blessed by a daughter who has reached amazing heights that no one ever thought possible. She still has challenges, but we face them together knowing we will find our way. I have had numerous gifts bestowed upon me, and they never cease. I am doubly blessed because now I have the honor of working with many other children, teens, and adults with ASD, and their families.

I am thankful to have found my true calling in life. It allows me to wake every day and say a silent thank you. Thank you for the gift of my daughter.

Autism, A Mother's Story
By Marion Pusey

Before Eric was born, I was a nurse specializing in premature babies i.e., working at Children's Hospital of Eastern Ontario (CHEO) in the Neonatal Intensive Care unit. Everything changed when Eric was born. Eric was born with Autism but I could not get a diagnosis until he was 5 1/2 years old. His diagnosis was "Autism with severe global delays." My nursing career ended so I could take care of Eric.

My sons Eric and Shaun became my life's work and through all my experiences (a lot of nightmares and horror stories). My passion has been to help other families so they won't have to experience the same frustrations, nightmares and heartache that I have gone through. I figured that I could best contribute to the growing Autism community by helping to provide visual resources, i.e., Picture Card

Communication, and to be a supporting friend to other families who have loved ones with Autism or other special needs.

Eric started speaking his first words around five years old, e.g. "milk" and "juice." Up until around eight or nine years old, he was scholastic, repeating everything he heard without showing and signs of understanding what he had said. Not having hardly any resources in Ottawa except the early form of ABA/IBI, I had to go a lot on instinct. From the very beginning, I kept talking to Eric and described everything we did and saw. I figured that I did not know how much Eric was taking in even though he couldn't talk. As I found out years later, Eric was remembering what I had said and done.

Eric was tactile defensive and had to learn about touch, textures, etc. He also had to get used to different sounds, volume, intensity, sudden noises like balloons popping, school bells, etc. Eric also had Pica (he would mouth/put everything in his mouth), *but* I had an extremely hard time feeding him. No doctors understood the feeding problem and blamed it on Autistic behaviors!! As it turned out, we finally found out when Eric was eight years old that his stomach wasn't formed properly and he had to have surgery to rebuild it. Eric did not have the ability to let us know how he as feeling physically and emotionally.

Everything that Eric has learned had to be broken down into small steps. When Eric was around seven years old, I took him to Beavers (part of the Cub Scouts/Brownies/Girl Guides organizations). My instinct was to try to socialize him within the community. Eric was a pilot project because none of the leaders knew anything about Autism. Also, Eric had a very few words and no give and take conversation. On one of our outings with the Beavers, we went to a wave pool with a big water slide. Eric kept on pulling at my leg and pointing to the water slide. I did not know at the time that Eric could not "generalize" i.e. whatever happens to other people coming off the water slide would happen to him. I decided that with Eric's interest still there after watching about 30 people going under him up at the bottom of the slide, well, we both went under water. All the way home, Eric kept repeating brand new words, "NOT FAIR! NOT FAIR!" The next day, Eric picked up a pencil and paper and started drawing water slides. Water slides have become one of Eric's intense interests. He can draw them to photographic detail and quality. I figured out how, with Eric's intense interest in water slides, to take his interest and use it as a learning tool to grow and expand on. To this day Eric's love of water slide parks and amusement parks is so strong that he is taking courses at college so he can design and build them.

Eric has three unusual savant skills: art, math and music. Eric started playing the piano incredibly well, perfect pitch and ear, all of a sudden. He had never had a lesson—he just sat down and played! He played piano (and now keyboards) so he could describe his feelings about water slides through music. Eric can sit down and play any music he hears and likes within five minutes!

Six years ago, Eric could not understand or handle the world becoming more complex. The schools believed in (forced) integration i.e. "no choice" and that Autistic children would become "normal" if they were around normal children. The schools never had enough money for a teacher's aide for Eric. In grades six and seven, Eric had to share a teacher's aide with six other children throughout the school. The teachers did not have a clue about autism and I as a parent was not allowed to go in to help. The teachers did not adapt what they taught—more visuals, letting Eric use "point form," giving Eric copies of the notes, etc. Eric became extremely aggressive, becoming a danger to himself and everyone around him. He would be sent home—expelled from school—at least once or twice a week, if not more because of "no violence tolerance." The Children's Aid Society said that they would help us only in an extreme crisis.

That crisis happened when we changed a routine slightly and Eric attacked his younger brother. I peeled Eric off his brother, and then Eric continued attacking me. Eric's brother ran upstairs and called "911" and Eric was taken to CHEO. All the doctors and Eric's Neurologist would do is "drug him out" and send him home. Or I could take him to the Robert Smart Center. Eric spent a week there and then was transferred into "the cottage program" which was a part of the Royal Ottawa Hospital. Eric spent six weeks in the "cottage program" where they tried giving different medications to Eric to see what would be most effective. The ROH staff knew nothing about Autism!

During this whole nightmare, the Children's Aid Society found a placement for Eric with Bain Croft Residential Services. Bairn Croft staff specialize in children and young adults who are on the ASD spectrum, or have any communicating, developmental and/ or social delay or disorder. Each child's care and programming are considered a major need in the child's life and are included in the "plan of care." Eric comes home to us on weekends and holidays and under Bairn Crofts care and guidance over the last six years he has flourished. He has learned "skills of daily living"; he is now living semi-independently, has graduated from the Precision Machining Technology Program at Algonquin College, plays bowling with Special Olympics, has a job, has a girlfriend and has many friends. By the way, if these kids do make it through to college, Algonquin College makes any adaptations necessary for the "special needs students" to be successful. They have been amazing with Eric! Eric is very happy and very proud of his achievements and we are extremely proud of him.

Through all this, Eric has become verbal.

The Gifts of Autism
By Jennifer Guthrie

I am a mother of four children with disabilities. These disabilities include both autism spectrum disorders and deafness. Two of my four children have an ASD. Three of my four children are deaf and wear cochlear implants. Each of them has touched me, my husband and everyone they have met in profound ways. They are brilliant, sweet, innocent and often hysterically entertaining. They have taught me and each other as much as they have learned themselves. I am so proud to call myself their mother and to have been given the gift of having them as my children. My life has meaning because of them.

The article I am writing focuses on the gifts associated with autism. My nine-year-old son, Christopher, has Asperger's Syndrome and my seven-year-old son, Daniel, has PDD NOS, as well as a severe /profound neural hearing loss and auditory neuropathy spectrum disorder. He wears bilateral cochlear implants. Christopher and Daniel have 2 ½-year-old twin brothers with the same hearing loss as Daniel. They also wear cochlear implants.

My son, Christopher, is brilliant. He excels in almost everything he does without trying. He is a perfectionist and at times his own worst enemy. This perfectionism is also what drives him to go above and beyond. He is also very creative. He plays the violin and is also a very talented artist, especially when it comes to creating comics. His ability to succeed with such little effort in so many things astounds me as is his ability to grow and mature.

This year he chose to play the violin and join his school chorus. His reasoning for chorus was to get over his fears. I was hesitant at first to allow him to take on so many additional responsibilities for fear of burning him out but he has handled them all. He is also in the gifted and talented education program at his school. I am so proud of him for trying new things even if he has been discouraged by previous attempts in the past. So many things in life come easily to him yet he is still striving to meet the challenges.

Throughout the years, Christopher, has been known to give one-liners that we refer to as "Christopherisms." One evening Christopher wanted to go outside to play but it was raining. My husband told Christopher that he could not go outside because it was raining and he would get wet. Chris's response to the fact that it was raining: "Well, Dad, you have your opinion and I have mine." Although Christopher may not always understand why we find him funny, we have to laugh and smile. It is usually when he is trying to be serious that he has entertained us or charmed us the most with his clever wit. His creative nature doesn't just end with his conversations. His stories and animated characters that he draws for his pictures and comics are phenomenal. They have such life and animation, much like my Christopher. Christopher's memory is also amazing. He looks at something once and has it. I wish I had his gift of recollection. I often find myself wishing that I had written more down as I forget more and more as the years go by. Sometimes, so much happens with my children that I'm afraid if I stop for too long to write about it or record it then I'll miss living in the moment and enjoying them.

My son, Daniel, works harder than anyone I know. He is patient and persistent. He is also loving, kind, quick to forgive and very protective of his brothers. Daniel couldn't fit in the world of hearing loss due to his autism and couldn't fit in the world of autism due to his hearing loss. He has always been caught somewhere in between. Due to his late diagnoses of hearing loss he did not communicate with anyone for two years and no one was successfully communicating with him. We did not know that he was deaf so we interacted with him the way a hearing parent with a hearing child would, through oral language. When Daniel was diagnosed first with hearing loss then autism, we began to use every method possible to get him to communicate in order to make up for lost time. We tried PECS, real pictures, sign, music and oral language. Pictures helped with Daniel's transition but ultimately he chose oral language. If you would look up deafness and autism, or deafness and cochlear implants, you would find virtually no information if any on a child with autism and deafness using oral language as their means of communication. Daniel pioneered the use of oral language and cochlear implants with an ASD diagnosis. I had no references. I had no resources. I had to make my own. There were no boundaries because it was rarely done. I even attended an educational conference where a hospital stated that you could not implant a child with auditory neuropathy and then later stated that a child with autism who had been implanted has very little chance of success. Well, my little chatter-box would prove both of their theories wrong. I stood up and did prove them wrong.

I always say that Daniel works twice as hard to get half as far as everyone else. That is not meant to be negative in any way. It just shows how hard this child has worked. He has not one but two diagnoses. He had no language for almost two years and he hears through the use of cochlear implants. He communicates orally and has been interacting with his peers this year, which is really exciting. I wasn't sure if his language delay was going to inhibit his ability to interact, but again, Daniel has risen to the occasion. He always surprises me by his dedication and he never gives up. He may get frustrated at times but he is always willing to try again. Daniel enjoys sports and loves being active. He also loves art, reading and is very creative when writing.

Both of my sons love their younger brothers and try their best to entertain and teach them. Brandon and Nathan love them dearly and learn so much from them. Christopher's progress and success comes from his willingness to try again each day. He truly enjoys life as does Daniel. All of my boys do. They are four of the happiest children I have ever met. They greet each day with a smile and on most days, a song. I have to add that while writing this, Christopher came home from school and immediately asked how Daniel was feeling because he had been home sick from school today. That just shows his sweet nature to put the concerns for his brother before anything else. Also, as I was reviewing this piece Daniel asked what I was writing about and I told him. He noticed at the top of my paper, that I had written "The Gifts of Autism" and he asked what gifts were. Then he asked, "Are Gifts from Jesus?" and I said yes. They are such sweet boys and they truly love, unconditionally with an innocence that I wish we all had. And I hope that innocence never leaves them.

Daniel, I believe, has made the most progress, not because of us or his education but because of what he learned from Christopher. Christopher was the first to truly engage him. Christopher was the first person he began to talk to and with. I'm not saying that the fantastic people who have worked and are currently working with Daniel have not made a lasting impression upon his development and achievements. But I credit Christopher for pulling Daniel out of his world and into ours. Daniel has in turn passed on a gift as well. He gave us the opportunity to diagnose Brandon and Nathan immediately with additional testing as all three children passed their newborn-hearing screening. This gave them the most precious gift. They had early access to sound and oral language and are making huge gains daily. I have Daniel to thank for that.

My boys have taught me patience, even on those days when I have none. They have taught me flexibility. They have taught me to slow down and enjoy the gifts that have been given to me and how my life has changed because of them. It wasn't the path that

I had chosen for myself, but the path that God has chosen for me. I truly believe that they saved me. They also made my marriage to my husband stronger. We were forced to truly rely on each other and communicate. With the addition of our twins in our already hectic life as well as their diagnoses and impending surgeries, we didn't know how we were going to make it. We kept asking why each time a new hurdle was thrust upon us. We had to stop asking why. This wasn't something that was done to us. It was something that was given to us. It was a gift. Nothing worth having is ever easy. It takes work and dedication. We do WORK daily. When we are tired, when we've had enough, when we have nothing left to give, we work.

I believe that there are no boundaries for my children, no limits. My motto has always been, "Let's try it." If it doesn't work, then we've tried and we will try something different. It's not about us, it's about them. This is their path. We are simply giving them the tools to get there.

I often find myself feeling sorry for the people who take pity on us or don't understand why we do what we do for the sake of our children. They don't understand what we've been given. Our life is not easy. Their lives are not easy. But, again, I will say that *nothing worth having is ever easy*. But it is worth it.

Addie's Story
By M. Moon

It was a beautiful spring day. She was a scheduled Cesarean Section, due to her brother's very difficult delivery. On April 11, 1984 Adria Elaine Moon was born to two adoring parents and one delighted big brother. During next two weeks we celebrated Jesus' triumphant entry into Jerusalem, His crucifixion on the cross and His glorious Resurrection. We felt incredibly blessed as God grew our family.

Adria (Addie) developed beautifully and grew by leaps and bounds over the next few months. We watched closely as all milestones were met. As a former teacher, I checked each milestone closely on the baby calendar. At five months, Addie was ahead of schedule and life was good.

At five-and-a-half months, Addie went to the doctor for her third DPT shot. She had been fussy with the first two shots in the series, but no one was prepared for the severe reaction Addie experienced within two hours of her third shot. The weekend was something I pray no one ever has to experience. Witnessing your child experience brain damage is almost more than one should ever endure. The Sunday after the shot, Addie was baptized at church. As I held my child before God, I ask His healing hand be placed on her small life. I knew Addie was forever changed from the shot. Little did I know the incredible impact that day would hold on the rest of our days.

In 1984 autism was not a word we knew. As a trained teacher, I had never seen a child with autism or even studied autism. It was a rare and unusual diagnosis. That diagnosis did not come easily. After the shot Addie did not sleep, fed every half hour, her body was stiff and made little or no eye contact, due to moving all the time. The constant moving started as a stiff arching, and progressed to constant fussing and moving. Addie immediately fell off the developmental chart and lost the ability to sit-up on her own. There was no language at a year and no language at two and then at three years. At two years of age, Addie began to walk, but from her very first step, she walked on her toes. As she struggled I prayed for Addie's healing.

The toddler years were painful for us. We searched for an answer, a plan of attack, a cure, all the while trying to have some sort of family life. Sleep deprivation ate away at our energy, our hope and courage. We traveled incredible miles seeing doctors, going to therapy, and attending an "at risk" preschool in another community. And I prayed for Addie's complete healing.

At six years of age, Addie entered our public school system as a "multi-handicapped" student. It was then that we first heard the diagnosis of autism. Public school was also the time and place we finally accepted Addie was "special" and made a conscious effort to learn and make her life better, within that diagnosis. This place of acceptance was a hard place to go. Acceptance meant, we had to let go of the "normalcy" in life we so desired. At this place called acceptance, there were no sleepovers, family vacations, prom dances, boyfriends, riding bikes, running, using silverware, language and so very much more. As we gave up all of these hoped-for joys, we gained endless therapy sessions, sleepless nights, rejection, people's rude stares, messes everywhere, hour upon hour of car rides, and hand over hand repetitive teaching of skills. It took us years to teach Addie to grasp a piece of food and hit her mouth. I worked for eight years to toilet train Addie. She would not allow us to hold her. I worked for years walking and rocking as I taught her to be held.

Comfort ... all children love to be comforted. Addie could not be comforted. Nothing we did seemed to ease her stress, stiff movements, and constant motion. She threw everything back over her shoulder as she bounced on her bottom, with head down. It took 10 years to teach her to throw forward. Toys were only there to throw. No developmental toy could be used as intended, it was merely thrown. The walls were damaged, the toys broken, and sleep deprivation continued ... and I prayed for Addie's healing.

As the years progressed we thought that things could get no worse. God had to see our suffering and bring some healing to our situation. Then puberty hit ... it was like an atom bomb going off in a war zone. Puberty brought "behaviors!" We thought autism, developmental delays and mental retardation were painful ... behaviors were torture.

During Addie's teen years she developed self-abusive behaviors. Addie screamed and beat her face with her open hand and at times, her fist. The schools had no clue what to do with behaviors. She was put in a quiet room and allowed to scream and beat herself for hours. After school she came home only to scream and beat herself another hour. She was withdrawn, dark and unhappy. I was on my knees begging God to bring joy to my child.

In the spring of 2001 I met a man who ran a summer camp for children with special needs. This kind man "knew" autism. He agreed to accept our Addie at his camp. This was the beginning of the long, but beautiful road to healing. The healing that God intended and planned for our child years before. This kind man taught me "behavior is language." He taught me Addie was speaking to us through her behaviors, and we started to listen. We learned she felt rejected and not a part of the group. Of course she did! Each time she struggled, she was put off by herself in a quiet room! While participating in "anything" was difficult, with such severe behaviors and fears, we learned she desired to be apart. Summer camp was based on love, acceptance and community outings. Addie began joining the community outings at camp by riding in her own car with a private one-on-one "age-appropriate" staff. If Addie was successful she stayed with the group, but if she began to struggle, her staff were there to support her through the behavior, and then bring her back to the group. Her camp friends learned to love Addie and accept her behaviors as she learned to love them and understand there were things in life she really enjoyed.

Addie participated in summer camp for nine summers. These were joyful summers as she learned, developed and blossomed into a young lady. Behaviors persisted, but we learned to understand them and through this understanding, reduce their severity and length. I thanked our faithful God for His grace and Love.

Today Addie is 29 years old and enjoys life. She still lives at home, but has her own "day house," where she spends time, after program, with her friends (her staff). With the support of the Medicaid IO Waiver, Addie is supported at home with private staff, hired and managed by our family. The Medicaid Waiver staff is an independent provider who works at our direction. While unique, this system allows us a high-quality staff and parental control. We have the ability to personally train staff with our own personal approach, set the schedule and direct all of Addie's outings. During the week she attends our county DD day program, where those important community outings are still a key part of her life.

God has used her unique life to touch others. Addie's grandmother suffers from dementia and many of the tools we use with Addie's communication issues are now useful with Grandma. While most of the family has become frustrated with her memory loss, we are able to approach her with the gentle tactics we have always used with Addie. It has worked beautifully, and allowed for a different, but quality relationship with Grandma in her later years. Addie's presence at our church has become an essential part of the worship experience. During the difficult years we learned that one safe place for Addie was our church. The church family has prayed and embraced Addie through the bad and now to the good. She is loved!

Is life easy? No! But is life blessed and the way God intended? Yes! Each day is a piece of the incredible journey God planned for our family. It is vastly different from the life I thought would be ours, but this life is rich and filled with understanding and patience taught by a most unlikely teacher: Addie. The lessons in Addie's life are those only taught through adversity and suffering. It's a journey of acceptance, repentance and priorities. Thank you Father God for the great honor of parenting your very special child.

Above: Ken's parents on their wedding day.
Below: Ken, proud mama and Leslie

CHAPTER 11

Living With Alzheimer's

The following are stories shared by families of people with Alzheimer's. Minimal editing has been done to preserve authenticity.

Momma Fern
By Leslie Stewart and Ken Routson

If I could only describe my mom in one word, it would be "Mommy." Being a mother was definitely her purpose, her passion, and her primary reason for living.

Mom was born Fern Hamilton on June 25, 1929, in Meigs County, Ohio, across the Ohio River from West Virginia. In fact, the day she was born, her father had to yell across the Ohio River to the doctor, who crossed the river in a rowboat to deliver her. My grandfather was 60 when my mother was born and had already brought nine children into the world and buried two wives.

My mom's purpose in life was to be a mother. She especially loved being a mommy to infants and would always light up whenever she saw small children. Mom, perhaps because of her abusive father, had much repressed anger that was expressed when her children would not obey her. Until her Alzheimer's symptoms became evident, she could be controlling, which I believe was due to her conditioning from a controlling and, at times, abusive father (unfortunately, like many from my parents' generation.) Even with those limiting characteristics, Mom was a great, caring mother. She and my dear father wanted to provide their children with all the wonder-filled things of life that they were denied as children themselves.

It was amazing that, with just an elementary school education and a rural childhood, my mother was so cultured and very aware of current events. She loved to read books to her children and would always scrape enough money together for her and her children to see the latest Disney movie. My parents sacrificed much time and money to give their children so much. They would rarely buy clothing for themselves, and although I think my dad would have enjoyed getting a babysitter and doing something fun with my mom, she would insist on staying home with us children. I believe during my entire childhood, my parents only went out twice. Besides her having an innate and intrinsic propensity for and love of music, I believe it was my mom's constant playing of the music of the 1940s that influenced my appreciation for what I deem to be "good music."

Mom was a devout Lutheran, and she had an intense fear of cancer—and I believe of death itself. Perhaps this fear of death was due to her own mother dying of a bleeding goiter when my mom was only nine years old.

Mom first exhibited signs of Alzheimer's in her early seventies. She went through what appeared to be days of depression. She rarely left the house, usually living in her nightclothes, and she kept the drapes closed, casting the house into darkness. I am not sure if there were environmental reasons for her depression—it could have been partially due to the deep debt she was getting into with the number of home equity loans she was taking out for house repairs. However, the depression may have been a continuation of the emotional challenges she had encountered throughout her life. Or maybe it was the ongoing effects of being taken to Dayton, Ohio and raised by a much older sister, and then her sister's husband when her mother died.

Mom eloped with my dad at 17, when he became her emotional security. Although she was fiercely independent in so many ways, she was always more or less emotionally terrified and emotionally dependent.

For example, I have many memories as a child of her fainting when she didn't get her way. My dearest father should have received an award for his unwavering patience and unconditional love and allowance! In fact it was that same unconditional love that I tried to lovingly bestow upon my dear mom before the Alzheimer's, but especially after.

My mother could be controlling and critical with her children like many parents of that era, and she often tried to manipulate us even after we left home as adults. I was able to set boundaries, and eventually she discovered that even her guilt-based threats couldn't manipulate me. Consequently, we developed a stronger, close bond.

Over the years, Leslie and I really enjoyed our visits and travels with mom. I will forever be grateful for her teaching me the importance of books and the power and beauty of music and nature. After I made peace with the loss of my "original mom" to Alzheimer's, that close bond became even more fortified. From this unconditional acceptance, we embarked on a magical journey into new dimensions!

Ken's spiritual partner Leslie's perception of Fern's Changes

From the very beginning of my relationship with "Momma Fern," she treated me kindly and was always my ally; it seemed I could do no wrong in her eyes. She was a wonderful blessing to me. I did not endure the usual childhood difficulties that the "real children of the house" had endured, so my perception of her is one of joy and love and acceptance, even if I was in a bad mood or not as cooperative as I could be.

Ken's dad passed on in 1982, after which Ken and I would spend every other Saturday at Fern's house. We felt it would be beneficial to her to keep her busy. She had just retired from Miami Valley Hospital, and she loved going on outings, home tours, and small weekend trips with us. She loved nature and history, so many times we would take historical adventures to places she had always wanted to visit but didn't feel she'd had the time or money for—for example, the home of Thomas Edison, the Longaberger Basket company in Newark, Ohio, and New York City.

On occasion, we would go to her home on our usual Saturday, and we would be able to tell the tone of the day by the way she would answer the door. If she would come to the door with her hair all messy, still in her nightclothes and sighing, we would know it could potentially be a very long afternoon. Ken, however, had a knack for turning situations around, and sometimes we could get her talked into at least getting out of the house for a while. Other times, there would be nothing—and I mean nothing—that could change her mind. She could be very obstinate!

After 25 years of our visits, we started noticing new and unusual behaviors. For example, she would hide her purse. Although we were not sure why she was hiding it, we would look and look and look and never to find the purse. We would just say that it was okay and that she would not need it that day anyway, which she would be fine with at first. But then she would suddenly become angry with not only us, but also herself over why she could not find it. We would try to redirect the conversation, which usually did the trick.

Around that time, she would occasionally lose her balance and fall more frequently. One time, Ken's sister came home and found Fern at the bottom of the staircase—she had fallen down the flight of stairs. No one was sure how long she had been lying there. She would often "forget" to eat, or if you asked her what she had had for lunch, she would not be able to even tell you if she had eaten at all. She would have severe bouts of vertigo, and someone would find her passed out in different areas in the home. It was becoming more and more apparent that she would need further assistance sooner rather than later. Ken and his siblings held a discussion, and decided it was time to move her into an assisted living arrangement.

After Fern settled into assisted living, she became yet another version of Fern. She insisted that she had to work, which to her meant assisting the activity director. We found it very beneficial for her to think this activity was "her job" because it gave her a sense of purpose.

During the first phase of Fern's Alzheimer's, we noticed new detail-oriented behaviors, such as methodically washing each dish one at a time, rinsing it, and then doing it again, and then lining up the glasses and dishes in neat rows. With this same precision and concentration, she would make her bed, ensuring all ends were properly tucked in. She was never like this before the Alzheimer's: she would allow dishes to stack up in the sink and maybe wash them once a week, and her bed was never made.

Another change I noticed was that when we asked her if she was ready to go somewhere, she would say yes, even though she was very unkempt in mismatched clothes with her hair a total mess and no makeup on. This was so very much out of character for Fern because she loved to be neat and clean and dressed very nicely with her hair just so and in makeup even if she were only going to the grocery. We discovered that it was just easier on everyone to not argue with her but allow her to be herself—so what if the clothes did not match? We said, "Wow, this is a whole new side of her."

We also noticed that she was less controlling, more spontaneous, and very witty! Ken and I would discuss how in-the-moment she was, how loving and affectionate, how she could go with the flow and ease of life—and we would say perhaps these are little lessons for ourselves as well. One of the greatest gifts that we eagerly looked forward to every Saturday was taking Mom for a ride. No matter what mood she was in, when we picked her up, she would become either as excited and exuberant as a child, or serene and harmonious, almost in a meditative state, as she gazed in wonderment at her surroundings. At times, she was ecstatic as she enthusiastically and vividly described the scenery, such as the clouds, cars, or people.

During other times, she would be very quite, serene, mellow, and non-communicative with words, but more with feelings. The feelings were transferred to us in a way that absorbed us and gave us a real sense of peace, tranquility, and love. At these times, we felt so one with her that it was as if we had all became one being. Even now, several years after her death, we can feel her presence at times, especially when we go for rides.

Unfortunately, all good things must come to an end, and when it became time for us to return her to her place of residence, she would become agitated. It was extremely difficult not only for her, but for us as well. The peace that once was would become in Fern anger, frustration, and loneliness tinged with helplessness and worry.

This type of shift in mood is why it is so important for care providers to learn how to nurture and redirect anxious and agitated people by establishing rapport and cultivating an interactive atmosphere of trust and unconditional love and acceptance. One of the gifts of Alzheimer's is the short term memory—if the person is gently redirected, they will often forget their previous experience or event and come into the moment with their new activity.

Momma Fern's Alzheimer's taught me that life doesn't have to be over if we receive a bad diagnosis. My new relationship with her afforded me new adventures and splendid simplicities, such as not worrying about others' perceptions, being more spontaneous, and being more alive and full of joy for each and every moment of the day! Also seeing things as if for the first time and experiencing the excitement you feel upon each and every "new discovery" in every-day experiences that you might have taken for granted only a moment prior. Momma Fern would see, feel, and hear things that we overlooked. In a bucket of garbage, she would discover delightful things after just picking something up, examining it, and processing it. A compact disc holder held delight for her as she would try to tear it apart to see how it was made. The most mundane detail to us was a brilliant new discovery for her. It was such a gift and delight to be with her and watch her discover something "new" each and every moment. Thank you, Momma Fern, for the gifts of living in the moment, cherishing each and every moment, and loving life as if it were your first, last, and only!

Caught Between Realities
By J.V. Potocny

Come with me into my world of Alzheimer's, to help learn the joy, pain and peace that one can find. By the way my name is Joe, yes simply Joe. I am a sufferer of Alzheimer's (AD) and Frontal Temporal Dementia (FTD). In other words, my brain does not function like yours. But that is ok, I live in a multiple of realities, unlike you, I never know when I will pop in or out of any of them.

My life is kind of like Bugs Bunny having Elmer Fudd chasing after him. I pop up in one place, than another and so on, until I find you. However I cannot dig holes to go into; I would wind up falling in them. See, this life presents many problems but one has to find the humor in it or just totally give up.

What you need to realize is that there is *no cure, no treatment (of value) and no known cause* for these diseases. Yes, that is right Virginia, we all DIE from this disease. Life expectancy is about two to ten years from diagnosis, more or less. Remember AD, FTD and other forms of dementia are not forms of *mental illness*, they are *diseases*. Our physical brains actually shrink and loose functionality.

It is my personal opinion that AD and other forms of dementia are auto immune diseases. I base this on the fact that the body, for whatever reason, causes the formation of the protein strand that becomes part of the beta amyloid protein, the suspected culprit in this disease. Just a little note—these amyloids can cause heart attacks, kidney failure, and liver problems. In other words, they can affect many organs throughout the body besides the brain.

We who suffer from this disease get to meet new people almost daily, even in our own households. Kind of like an emu, who turns around to look at the same person and sees a new person, a new friend. We get to forget the past gradually, the good stuff to be sure, but also the pain caused by others in our lives and ourselves. We get to forget all the nonsense we were taught. The birds, clouds, trees and such all take on a new meaning in the world we are thrust into.

If you are reading this and saying to yourself, right this guy is ok, I want you to know that spell checker and grammar checker are wonderful. See if I chose not to use them, as I do on my blog, you would need to learn how to Speak Alzheimer's. My dialect is known as *joeneese*, yes all my own a mix of various words, utterances, looks and whatever else comes along.

Most people wonder how one handles getting this news. Well let me tell you some go to pieces, some cry, some get angry, some wonder why me, etc. Me, I just said thanks now you have confirmed what I have thought for the past 10 years or so. See I suffered from what I now call *DDSS* or better known as *Depressed Distracted Stress Syndrome*. I have found over the years since 2004 that many people with AD went through the same annoying diagnosis when they knew the doctor was off the beam so to speak if not outright crazy. To be validated was a relief to me, not a blow to my life. Actually being given this death sentence relieved me of some fears of death. See I never feared dying but I did fear death from a heart attack or that nanosecond between life and death as we call it. But suddenly that no longer bothered me. It just went the way of a wind storm puff.

I am not a religious person, so let us get that out of the way, but I do believe in one God and Jesus Christ. See I look at myself as a Spiritual Being Having a Human Experience. Let me tell you, it has not been fun or comforting, really until now. I know I am leaving here and that is ok now, where I will wind up we will see. I do have places I go to now but I doubt that is where I will end up, although I would not mind.

Some of the humorous things I find is my wife calling me, Joe, Joseph, Joseph where are you, and turn to her and say, "What?" rather with a little terseness; see she has called me back from where

I was. She asks me who have I been talking to and where was I. By this time I have no idea of what the heck she is talking about, because it is gone from me. She tells me I was sitting there talking and moving my hands and looking out as if I could see who it was. Maybe she should join the conversation, who knows what might take place. Some of our family discussions at the dinner table are just, well right out of a sitcom. For me especially because it does not take long for me to get lost in them and not know what is going on, let alone why I have this plate of stuff in front of me. I even laugh at myself when I fall. Everyone gets so concerned and all I do is lay there and laugh. See I find these things to be funny, why because I am laughing at myself and my own stubbornness at times. Like climbing on a ladder, no business being on one, and the next thing I know the ladder went for a walk and I met the floor on my back and head.

Do not get the wrong idea, this world of Alzheimer's and other forms of dementia are without a doubt terrifying. Not only to those who take care of us, and we can be a real handful to deal with, but to us that wander in the fog of it. See we not only have to try and live in your reality, but we are forced into a different reality, the World of Dementia: a life of continual forgetfulness and being lost and not knowing where you are one minute to the next. Filled with frustration, aggravation, not being able to do the things you once could. Sitting down to do something and there you sit because you do not have a hint of what it was you were going to do. I had to take a break from this for a couple of hours, because my brain hurt and stopped talking to my hands and I did not know what to write or say. I do know one thing that someday I will be set free from this life of different Joe's and be just Joe in yet another reality.

Joe & Helen: A Lifetime of Memories United by Love
By Ellen Belk
I was in New Jersey visiting one of the communities that I supported as a Divisional Director of Memory Care. This particular space had a calm, soothing and welcoming vibe filled with residents from very diverse backgrounds.

There were several veterans, former schoolteachers and a former New Jersey Highway Patrolman. The Patrolman had survived an entire career keeping the roads of New Jersey safe. Yet, here he was, still regal and stoic and now living with Alzheimer's disease. The cruelty of the disease, often takes my breath away—and I've been doing this work for nearly 13 years. Unfortunately, it never gets easier.

However, I decided early in my career to focus on all the amazing things I can still learn from the folks with the disease. And, trust me the lessons are endless.

On this Jersey visit while I stood in the main living room chatting with Rachel the director, we were approached by a gentleman. His smile was quick and his handshake was strong. Rachel introduced me to **Joe** and quickly mentioned that the flame red Jaguar in the parking lot belonged to him.

I had but a mere second to come up with a snappy comeback.

You see, in the "World of Alzheimer's" it's a thin line between the real truth and the "fuzzy-jumbled-vague" memories. So, as a trained professional, I'm an expert at "being in the moment" with anyone I meet within the secured walls of a Dementia unit. Some days a *wrinkled-faced-senior* will ask for their mother or confuse me with being a relative. And, that's okay.

I simply "roll-with-it." Which means to *be-in-the-moment* with them. The theory is, to minimize the anxiety and fear that goes along with losing your memory, it's best to let the person with the impairment be **who** they think they are and let them be **where** they think they are.

So, here I stood shaking hands with **Joe** and being told that his red Jaguar was in the parking lot. I smiled and said, "Gosh, don't we *all* wish we had a red Jaguar." Rachel piped up quickly, "No seriously, Joe has a red Jaguar, he goes out every morning for the paper and coffee."

Wow, either this was the most Liberal secured Dementia Unit on the East Coast or, there was another explanation.

Rachel explained. **Joe's** wife **Helen** had Alzheimer's and instead of leaving her alone in this Dementia unit, **Joe** had decided to move in with **Helen**. "We've been married over 55 years," **Joe** remarked. "I'm not about to let her go now."

The lump in my throat was overpowering.

It was then, that I met **Helen**. She was a pint-sized, lovely lady with an impish grin and amazingly bright blue eyes. Her well-maintained hair was thick and white. She was a bundle of energy and a bundle of words. She was drawn to me immediately. I realized in a split second why it would be hard to be apart from her.

First, she complimented me on my blouse. "I just love what you are wearing," she cooed. "It's a lovely color on you." I loved **Helen** instantly!

She and **Joe** stood close to each other and spoke over one another as they both brought me "up-to-date" on their marriage and life journey. I learned that they'd never had children, that **Joe** worked for the Post Master General and that their wedding ceremony was at a Roman Catholic Church near the Jersey Shore.

It was time for lunch. **Joe** took **Helen** by the hand and guided her to their appointed table. He helped her order her meal and kept the table laughing with various quips and witty comments. I was in awe of his commitment to stand by his wife through this chapter of their life journey.

After lunch, for some reason, still unknown to me, **Helen** was drawn right back to my side. She complimented me on my blouse again. And stood close as she shared, in great detail, a story about the children that her nephew and his wife had adopted. She was animated as she chatted about the children and the various countries that they were from. I was mesmerized by her.

Joe stood nearby, with a loving smile on his face, he nodded his head and was equally as absorbed in the story **Helen** was telling. She continued giving exquisite details about both children and their countries. "That's amazing," I said. "Which countries are the children from, Helen?"

Helen came up for air for a brief second as she pondered the answer.

I turned to **Joe**. He shook his head and muttered gently, for only my ears to hear, "I have no idea what she's talking about."

I turned back to **Helen**, who was unfazed and non-pulsed. She was back into story-telling mode and didn't skip a beat. Again, I had to swallow hard as I tried to compose myself. **Joe** was so loving and so supportive. He was the *model* caregiver.

Selfishly, I wanted to take him on the road with me so that he could help me train all the paid professionals who didn't always seem to "get it" the way **Joe** clearly did.

He was living his life thru all of **Helen's** "moments."

My bond with **Joe** and **Helen** only deepened as they invited me into the room that they shared. I glanced around the tidy space. One twin bed on the left side with the other twin bed under the window. There were cherished possessions and pictures properly placed about, playing witness to a life that was fully lived.

Joe and I sat on the bed, under the window while **Helen** stood close by. She continued to speak quickly, sharing super-clear details about their wedding day. Joe handed me the amazingly well-kept wedding album. We flipped through the pages and I gazed at the black and white photos of the happy, smiling and much younger version of the two seniors that were with me now.

They looked like movie stars! And, I told them so. "Oh, you can't imagine how good our photographer was," **Helen** said. "**Joe**, what was his name again?"

I held their photo album in my hand and turned the pages gingerly as both **Joe** and **Helen** shared stories and details about every picture. I was completely captivated.

Twenty minutes later, I stood to leave. **Helen** thanked me for stopping by. "I know you have such a busy schedule," she commented. I smiled down lovingly at tiny Helen.

Clearly she didn't know my schedule; she didn't even know who I really was or what I did for a living. But she continued to amaze me with her steady stream of clear, concise language that was surprisingly coherent for someone with Alzheimer's disease.

I thanked them for the visit from the bottom of my heart. **Joe** turned his back for a moment and opened up a dresser drawer. "Here," he said, "Please take this. You've been so kind to us; I want you to have it,"

"Yes, please, you must take it" **Helen** chirped.

Joe handed over a blue fleece scarf, neatly folded, that still had the sales tag attached. "**Joe**, really, you don't have to give me anything," I said.

"Please, I insist. I know you are busy and you've been so kind"

"Would you like something to drink?" **Helen** offered.

I reached for the scarf and clutched it to my chest. At that moment in time it was the greatest gift anyone had ever bestowed upon me.

I was near my breaking point. I'd swallowed lumps in my throat and bitten back tears all day as I struggled to remain professional. These two had completely touched my heart. My eyes glazed over as I stood in their one room space filled with 55 years of treasures. I hugged them both and promised to visit again, someday soon.

I handed the lovely blue fleece scarf to Rachel as I prepared to leave. She promised to discretely put it back in Joe's drawer later.

As I boarded the plane to fly back to my home I silently reflected on the power of **Joe's** devotion to **Helen.**

Joe's ability to live-in-the-moment with **Helen** make her remaining days on earth as lovely as possible was inspiring.

I hugged my husband extra tight that evening.

Ellen Belk, President, Keep In Mind, Inc. and creator of Memory Magz. www.keepinmindinc.com

Aunt Eva Townsend
By Barbara Brand

This is about a wonderful woman that I had in my life for 57 years. She was my mother's younger sister. She was never blessed to have any children of her own, so her nieces and nephews were her children. She would do everything for us and spoil us, even children in her church. She was a very active woman who loved to fish, sing, play piano and sang in the church choir, and was also a Sunday school teacher.

My Aunt Eva was diagnosed with Alzheimer's. It really hurt us, because here was a lady who was healthy, cheerful, lively, very giving and loving. She had Alzheimer's for fifteen years before dying. In fact, after her Alzheimer's she couldn't remember a lot of things, but she would always be able to remember her favorite gospel music, especially "How great thou art." She remembered that song until the day she died.

My Aunt always said that God would have to catch her when it was her time to go, but one day, she got tired and went to sleep with the lord. We miss her dearly but she was awaiting Gabrielle to blow his trumpet.

Although Alzheimer's can be a terrible disease, it was a blessing, because in October of 2001 when her sister (my mom) died, it broke her heart. They had been so close all their life talking on the phone every day. Aunt Eva got Alzheimer's shortly afterwards and although Alzheimer's is hard on the people who have to take care of them, the Alzheimer's was a way of soothing her grief and pain. My auntie worried less and became even closer to God. My Auntie's Alzheimer's and the death of my first grandchild, only two years old, from a heart defect, gave me the gift of importance of family. It taught me to savor life and live it to its fullest while I can, and to spend quality time with loved ones because you never know how long you will have them with you.

The gifts I received from her disease were for me to savor the precious time we have with our loved ones, to spend quality time with the people we love, and enjoy each and every moment to the fullest!

Barbara Brand, the niece who loved Aunt Eva dearly.

Ruth's Story
By Dennis Beery

My mom was one of the most annoying people I knew. She couldn't leave anything alone that might possibly benefit from her advice. This pretty much included everything, whether she knew anything about it or not. My friends even commented, just out of amazement.

She was also a huge worrier and fearful of any new undertaking. She always thought of something that could go horribly wrong. As a kid my most common warnings were that something might put my eye out or break my back and leave me paralyzed for life. Her warnings changed to match my age as I got older but weren't any less dire. After I moved out and got married she would send me articles cut out of newspapers that told of even more things that could go wrong. She would write and underline "Watch out!" somewhere at the top of the section she'd cut from the page and then underline it, as though just the words "Watch Out!" might not catch my attention.

The topic of death was entirely taboo. She said she just couldn't talk about it and didn't want to think about it. Whereas most people find it at least interesting in maybe a religious or mystical sense, she just wouldn't go there at all. No use bringing that one up.

One day she called and said Dad, who had congestive heart failure, had gone into the hospital again for high doses of diuretics. He'd had to do this a few times before and mom and I thought I'd be more help if I visited them for a few days just as he was released. This had become the norm. Dad preferred me to visit when he was home, too. He hated the hospital.

When I knew when he was getting out I drove across Ohio to their home, unpacked and said hi to mom, and then went to the hospital to pick dad up and take him home. This time, though, when I helped him into the car he seemed a lot weaker than usual.

When we got home he barely made it up the 2 small steps from the garage into the kitchen. He couldn't walk without both a walker and help from me, had a prescription for an oxygen tank, and was incontinent. His doctor also gave him only two months to live, something she only told me. I went to a nursing home supply for equipment and supplies, called my employer and said I was taking a leave of absence and then settled in to assist mom and help with dad's care and his impending death from a heart too weak to pump the liquid from his lungs. He told me he had his fill of hospitals, dreaded nursing homes (mom did, too) and wanted to die at home if this was the time.

I stayed for two months until dad died one night in his Lazy Boy. I'd been sleeping on the couch in order to be with him when he died. He didn't ask me to and I'm still not certain that was what he wanted but it didn't seem right to let someone die alone if it could be avoided. I woke when dad suddenly sat up and moved the waste basket that was next to his chair, a completely meaningless act it seemed. He then sat back, I moved over next to him, his chest appeared to convulse a couple of times and he took a couple last breaths while I told him bye and put my hand on his head. He was never physically affectionate with me and I hoped that didn't feel awkward to him.

I sat with him in the living room for about an hour to adjust to what had just happened and then went to wake mom and tell her. Surprisingly she dealt with the whole thing pretty well. She cried but over the next few days moved on fairly quickly.

While staying with them I noticed mom's memory wasn't too good. I found piles of notes covering much of the kitchen counter, written on envelopes and scraps of paper. Most were duplicated in other notes and many were a year or two old. I noticed that lots of them were just things like a date and the note "Dennis called today," and other mundane events that had occurred, like a TV show she wanted to tell me about because she saw it and thought it was cute. It wasn't like she was just writing down things to do and then forgetting and writing it down again. It was a little like she was recording her life, her own history, and not throwing anything out. I also found things she'd written about people and events from years ago, small notes describing how various relatives were related, like she didn't want to forget.

In the following days I organized things for her, helped her do the income taxes, went through her papers, helped her throw out things she didn't care about, and set up an easy filing system for bills and other records. I helped her organize her medications (and threw out tons of expired ones) in a weekly planner so she always knew if she'd taken anything, instead of making or forgetting to make more notes.

I also condensed all her notes and threw out some each day that I thought would confuse her. She didn't seem to notice.

When she seemed to be doing pretty well and I knew she had some active support from a few neighbors and relatives I went back home.

Over the next two or three years I called her a lot and my wife and I visited a few weekends, certainly holidays. While there I would help keep her papers and appointments organized and would call and thank neighbors and relatives who helped her, trying to keep that network going by expressing my gratitude. Mom seemed to still be doing alright, mostly.

At home, though, I began to get calls from the neighbors and relatives who were checking in on her. They told me they were worried about her memory. Some were concerned about her driving. They didn't have anything specific to tell me; just that she seemed a lot more forgetful, but always added that she seemed to be doing ok.

I began to worry more. I thought at least she was in the small town she'd grown up in so I thought most things were covered by long-term memory. I worried over her driving, too, wondering when

I should step in and do something. I also noticed that she seemed far less worried and concerned about her diminishing memory than I was. She seemed a little lighter about things. That struck me as odd but it helped the situation.

One day I came home from work and found a phone message from the Highway Patrol in mom's part of the state. I felt a little panicky so I drank a glass of wine before I called them back. They said mom had run into the back of the car in front of her in a city about 20 miles from her home. No one else was injured but mom was banged up some and in the hospital there. Her Boston terrier, which had been her constant companion for probably what felt to her like 40 years (they had bought three of these dogs successively and given them all the same name), was being bordered by a vet. Dad had always driven when they went places and since his death mom got rides from one of my aunts who probably also shouldn't have been driving, to cover the few times she had to go out of town. The patrolman said she seemed confused as to why she was there.

I called mom at the hospital. She sounded surprisingly good in spite of an injured knee, and was worried about the dog.

I packed, drove there, got the dog and went to visit mom. She said she had just meant to go to the store a few blocks away but had gotten turned around and ended up 20 miles from home in a heavily-trafficked part of a large city where she never ever drove.

I called my wife. It seemed like mom finally couldn't live alone and we thought I should bring her home to live with us. We had tried to prepare for this. Being an only child, I thought it fell entirely to me to help. In spite of my mom making my wife miserable after we married, my wife was supportive and wanted to do the right thing.

After three weeks in the hospital, I brought mom to my own town, to a nursing home a few blocks away for about a month of rehab. We brought the dog home and took care of it. During this time I drove back and forth across the state, clearing out her house, packing things she wanted, and putting the house up for sale. Other than hating the nursing home, mom seemed to be taking this major change in her life pretty lightly. I was surprised by that. She didn't even seem to mind not driving any more.

After the month of rehab I moved mom into a guest room in our home. She had a lift chair and a walker, a good TV, and her dog. I took care of her affairs and doctor appointments and got her enrolled in a local elderly day program for two or three days a week for some activity and social contact beyond what I could provide. She mostly seemed to like it, coming home each day and telling me how stupid the other people were in contrast to herself and what they had for lunch.

I expected her to become depressed, having lost so much so fast, but it never came. She seemed just fine and happy to be taken care of, though I'd expected the opposite.

I saw a lot of change, which mostly seemed for the better. Mom always was afraid before, keeping curtains tightly closed at night so no one could see in but now she wasn't concerned with that. She was just as self-centered as always and still too interfering but less so, as if there wasn't as much worrying her now—less for her to interfere with. I heard of fewer things that could go wrong, less dangers. The always-looming, horrible injuries that so many activities could likely result in weren't mentioned anymore. She seemed mostly content to get out now and then and to sit with her bulldog at home and watch TV. She watched *House*, not because of the interesting plots but because he had pretty eyes. She didn't seem afraid anymore. She seemed simpler.

After about a year of my wife's increasing allergic reactions to mom's dog, I felt I had to pick between the dog living with us and my wife's ability to breathe. I dreaded this because the bulldog and its predecessors had been long-term companions but there weren't any more remedies to try. I explained this to mom. She cried for about two weeks, then came up with the suggestion that she move somewhere else where she could keep her dog. I checked around and was feeling pretty discouraged when my oldest daughter called with an idea.

Mom could move in with her and her two young daughters, about three hours away in Indiana. The dog could stay with mom and they could look after them both. My daughter could quit her job and I could pay her for mom's care while she went back to school. My younger daughter and her family lived in the same town and mom would be with her grandkids and great grandkids. My oldest daughter had once been a social worker in a nursing home and a case manager for developmentally disabled people and she thought it would be a perfect arrangement.

I tried to talk her out of it. I reminded her about mom's severely annoying qualities and self-centeredness but she insisted it was a good plan. We agreed to do it and mom said it was fine with her but I still wasn't sure it would work.

So we moved mom in with my older daughter and her two kids. Mom resumed being cared for and watching *House* with her dog. It worked out at first. It seemed healthy to have mom's grandkids helping their grandma and experiencing an extended family, etc. and the whole plan looked like it might work.

Gradually, though, mom began to get to them. Her memory loss progressed into obvious dementia. She would repeat herself constantly and having even fewer intact social graces, wouldn't hesitate to express opinions without any apparent appreciation of their effects on other people. On the other hand, though, we noticed that her sense of humor, appropriate or not, was stronger than ever. Other than the dog getting out and running away she didn't seem afraid of much else. In fact she didn't express much anxiety at all, whereas worrying had been a way of life for her before.

About a year later, when my daughter was beginning to express doubts about being able to continue this arrangement, my daughter called me. She said mom seemed much more out of it, sort of absent, and that she might be close to death. We should come really soon, she thought. My other daughter and her family were also alerted.

It was the week before Christmas. My wife and I had taken time off from work to stay at my daughter's house for the holiday so we packed and went a little earlier than we'd planned. We moved in with my daughter and her two girls and took turns sitting with my mom. She spent most of her time sleeping in her chair with one arm resting on her bulldog next to her. Other times she appeared to be in a half awake state talking to dead relatives, then falling asleep again. She was 88, had no interest in dying in a hospital, and was exactly in the situation I thought she would have wanted when she died—home with family, dog, and TV. We just waited and tried to be some company for her. She had a few lucid times, when we would watch TV with her or talk some.

After about three days she died sleeping in her lift-chair with her dog. We closed her eyes and tried to make her look comfortable and not scary. We talked to the grandkids and then brought them in to see her and let them adjust to this very different event before we called the police a couple hours later. They'd never seen a dead person before and were a little wary but more curious.

We had mom's body shipped back to her hometown to be buried next to my dad, and then got through Christmas together, after which we went back home to resume our lives. In my mind, things had been tough for everyone but worked out pretty well for mom.

My wife and I have since talked about how mom had changed as her memory loss had progressed more and more. On one hand mom had become even harder to be around. As her memory loss had progressed, what used to be conversation became constant repetition coupled with a loss of all restraints on her self-centeredness. Her hurtful, inappropriate, and insulting remarks seemed magnified by repetition and loss of any forethought.

However, it seemed to us that mom's progressing dementia had also caused something good to happen to her. The whole family had noticed her decreasing fears. She seemed afraid of far fewer things, which provided her with much less to caution others about. Most remarkable of all was that she appeared to have no fear of her impending death. I thought that being so close to the end of her life would have been obvious to her but we never saw any indication of concern. She expressed no fears of pain or hospitalization. She appeared free of existential worries. She also seemed satisfied with her much-reduced life and loss of independence, as though she didn't spend time using her past memories to bemoan her present condition. There was no sad reminiscing.

If dementia affects some parts of one's mind and perhaps not others, then it seems to me that mom got lucky. It was as if the parts of her mind that provided her the most fear and misery during her life had been the most affected and somewhat erased. During the end part of her life when she could have justifiably being the most terrified, she seemed by far the most content and unafraid. Things to fear and worry about were no longer on her mind, she appeared happy just to be around family, her snoring bulldog, and a decent TV. Right up until she died *House* still had pretty eyes and that was pretty much enough.

Down Syndrome And Alzheimer's
By Nancy Reder, RN

The National Association for Down Syndrome defines Down Syndrome as a genetic condition that causes delays in physical and intellectual development. It occurs in one in every 691 births. Persons with DS have 47 chromosomes instead of the usual 46. I like how this association emphasizes that individuals with Down are more like others than different. Many parents of older children with Down were told that their children would possibly die in their late thirties. Currently their life expectancy is 55 with some living in their sixties and a few seventies.

Studies suggest 75% of people with Down Syndrome 65 or older have Alzheimer's. Approximately six times greater than the public.

Research determines that even in the late thirties that the brains of those with Down have significant levels of plaques and tangles, that are indicative of Alzheimer's disease. Nevertheless not everyone with Down syndrome develop Alzheimer's symptoms.

Symptoms

In people with Down syndrome, changes in overall function, personality and behavior may be more common early signs of Alzheimer's than memory loss and forgetfulness.

Early symptoms may include:
- Reduced interest in being sociable, conversing or expressing thoughts
- Decreased enthusiasm for usual activities
- Decline in ability to pay attention
- Sadness, fearfulness or anxiety
- Irritability, uncooperativeness or aggression
- Restlessness or sleep disturbances
- Seizures that begin in adulthood
- Changes in coordination and walking
- Increased noisiness or excitability

Memory loss also may occur. Researchers do not yet know why early Alzheimer's symptom patterns may tend to differ among those with and without Down syndrome. (Source: Alz.org.)

One hypothesis for why Down syndrome individuals would be predisposed to developing Alzheimer's pathological changes is the observation that the gene that encodes the precursor of the amyloid protein is located on chromosome 21. An extra copy of this gene occurs in Down syndrome and may lead to "over production" of amyloid, and ultimately to its accumulation as senile plaques. (Source: Hyman, B T. Prog. clin. Biol Res. 1992; 379:123-42 Neurology Service, Massachusetts General Hospital, Boston 02114)

I first met Jodi, now age 46, through a volunteer experience called Friends by Choice, a collaborative effort between two residential providers in Dayton, Ohio. Jodi was born with down syndrome and now has Alzheimer's.

Both Resident Home Association and Choices in Community Living had observed residents being without family involvement due to a variety of reasons. Many residents wanted to make new friends and share time with someone special in their lives—a friend they could call their own. Thus, a collaborative effort matched volunteers with persons with developmental disabilities and my involvement began.

When I first met Jodi, who is essentially non-verbal and living with Down syndrome, she was non-communicative with me and unwilling to leave the protection of her group home and staff. Building rapport and trust was a challenge. My previous experience as an RN working and teaching in the field of Developmental Disabilities for many years had given me insight into her needs and the wisdom to take things slow. As time went by through visits to her home, walks, cookouts, eating out, and talking on the phone, she became comfortable with me in her life. A mutual friendship was forged!

Our phone conversations are a challenge—my talking and Jodi "grunting" replies. However, forty-eight years of marriage has prepared me well for this form of communication!

As the years began to pass and Jodi aged, the inevitable happened.

I spend three months in Florida and maintain phone contact with her. Upon my return last April, I noticed her change in mental status and ability to follow directions as we did artwork together.

An observant and caring staff along with a Home Manager as protective as a mother had advocated for an appropriate medical evaluation. A diagnosis of Alzheimer's had been given and medication implemented shortly before I had returned.

Jodi is responding well to medication and the continued love and understanding of her caretakers. She once again can enjoy the family environment of her home. The other three women in the home are her sisters and sometimes the "fur flies" as with all siblings.

When Jodi reaches out to touch my hand and gives me her smile, I find joy and purpose in my life the same as I do when my granddaughters reach out to me unconditionally.

As I write this, the holiday season is approaching. Her love of anything pink and Princess-themed makes it easy and a joy in gift giving. She shares her gifts with me with the same joy and pride. May we have many more opportunities to enjoy each other. She is one of my life teachers.

Jodi's gift to me is her trust—a fragile gift that could be shattered in a heartbeat. She gives me peace.

As a nurse working one of the many "hats" of my career, I was employed as an RN in a small nursing care facility. One of the experiences that has remained with me was an elderly woman, confused and alone, who would often become agitated. She would cry out, "My baby, my baby, I want my baby." Since I had no baby, live or doll-like to give her, I would roll up a thick towel and put it in to her arms, telling her, "Here is your baby." She would cuddle and sing to her "baby" and immediately start to calm down.

Such a simple act that brought joy to us both!

Growing up in the 40s and 50s in a small midwest town, I had been protected from the hidden challenges people often faced. "Differences" were not discussed, only hinted at. No children in any of my classes were labeled "disabled" or in the vernacular of the times, "handicapped." In my sheltered world they just didn't exist. I rarely saw anyone in a wheelchair—surely only people hospitalized needed such an assistive device, and then only for a short time.

As close as I came was a boy with Down syndrome in my grandparent's neighborhood. I knew he was different and I remember beating up on a couple of neighborhood boys who forced him to eat fishing worms. Not bad for a nine-year-old girl!

In my early adulthood, and I use that term loosely, I watched my as my grandfather developed Dementia, which was probably Alzheimer's. The family labeled it as "hardening of the arteries." He was a "pistol" as we say in Ohio. As I progressed in my professional career as a nurse and life in general, I began to realize that my formal and personal education were sorely lacking, let alone my knowledge about life in general. It was my goal and responsibility to rectify the situation, and I set out doing just that.

Life lands one on many paths and journeys, most surprises. As I found my way on that convoluted path through family practice, psychiatric, and geriatric nursing I was blessed to gravitate to the field of "disability care." To say I learned far more from the people who were differently challenged is a gross understatement.

I thank them, and my two granddaughters, for teaching and continuing to teach me in my twilight years, just what life is truly about.

My love of differences, natural curiosity, and penchant for thing "outside the box" will continue to present me with challenges to grow as a spiritual and caring human. I am flawed and in need of the journey my special friends will continue to grace me with.

Thank you, all my life teachers, and my gratitude to Ken for inviting on this journey.

CHAPTER 12

Extraordinary Gifts

One of my first experiences in observing an extraordinary gift was when I was developing foster care and monitoring apartment programs in the 1980s for Choices in Community Living in Dayton, Ohio.

Through the facility, I knew a young man with autism who required staff to enable him to live in an apartment that he shared with another person with developmental disabilities. One day this young man asked me when I was born, and I told him my birth date, which is February 2, 1952. Immediately he said, "You were born on a Saturday."

Then he asked, "When was your girlfriend, Leslie, born?" I replied, "January 27, 1953." He instantly reported that Leslie was born on a Tuesday. He asked about my mother as well.

I was astonished when my mom and Leslie both confirmed his accuracy on their day of birth! Then what was even more spectacular was that approximately ten years later, while Leslie and I were attending the Special Olympics, we ran into him. Not only did he remember our birth dates, but he said in his typical monotone voice, "Ken left Choices on September 29th, 1989." Wow! That indeed was the date I left Choices and the date of my going away party. It is amazing to me that he could remember such facts even with the number of staff that had come and gone from his home after I left.

I have rarely met a person with Asperger's who was not born with inherent talents and gifts such as the ability to draw or paint sophisticated and detailed pictures at an early age, calculate complicated mathematical problems, play instruments from instant recall, or write very sophisticated and lengthy musical compositions. At the very least, I have never known a person with Asperger's who didn't at least have a propensity to excel in certain areas or have abnormal obsessions (or a passion or interest) with something in particular. For example, those I've known with Asperger's have had keen interest in reptiles, maps, astronomy, mathematics, calendars, mechanical items, fictional characters, dinosaurs, television shows, personalities, and movies. In fact, they usually excel in their particular talent or gift, becoming an "expert" on that specific subject.

Persons who display savant tendencies typically have developmental disabilities such as autism or other conditions formerly referred to as "mental retardation." J. Langdon Down, after whom

Down syndrome was originally named, used the word "savant" to describe such giftedness in otherwise disabled individuals. However, there are also cases of people with brain injuries or disease that happen before, during, or after birth. Until I started my book research and read *Musicophilia: Tales of Music and the Brain* by Oliver Sacks or heard stories from family members and nursing staff, I had never heard of anyone with Alzheimer's or who had been struck by lightning developing savant characteristics. According to my research and reports from music and art therapists, many patients who were talented musicians and artists before their advanced dementia could still perform difficult musical pieces or art pieces astonishingly well even when they were incapable of memory or required total care. Even more surprising to me after reading several of Oliver Sacks' books were the stories from therapists around the world who knew of Alzheimer's patients with no prior particular talent who developed art or musical abilities *after* the Alzheimer's onset.

Anyone fascinated with musical savants or just the power of music in general should read Oliver Sacks' book *Musicophilia*. He talks about the "retarded man" he met who was not born with disabilities but contracted meningitis that resulted in mental disabilities, including spastic limbs and voice. Sacks said that this patient developed prodigious rote memory—especially musical memory. He referred to him having a "phonographic memory." He could listen to musical compositions and either sing them or play them back on the piano. Dr. Sacks said:

> *When I met him in 1984, he told me that he knew more than two thousand operas, as well as the Messiah, the Christmas Oratorio, and all of Bach's cantatas. I brought along scores of some of these, and tested him as best I could; I found I was unable to fault him. And it was not just the melodies that he remembered. He had learned, from listening to performances, what every instrument played, what every voice sang. When I played him a piece by Debussy that he had never heard, he was able to repeat it, almost flawlessly, on the piano. He then transposed it into different keys and extemporized on it a little, in a Debussyan way. He could grasp the rules and conventions of any music he heard, even if it was unfamiliar or not to his taste. This was musicianship of a high order in a man who was otherwise so mentally impoverished.*[1]

---

1   Sacks, Oliver, *Musicophilia* New York (Vintage Books Sept. 2008) Chap.12, P 163

Another similar story is that of Leslie Lemke. I will never forget when I saw Leslie on *60 Minutes* in the early 80s. Leslie was born with autism and glaucoma, and had his eyes removed after birth. Even though he had severe brain damage, autism, cerebral palsy, and was blind, he, like the young man in Sacks' example, could play flawlessly songs on the piano he had never before heard. When he was only 16, Leslie heard Tchaikovsky's Piano Concerto no.1 and was able to instantly play it back from memory!

In an interview with *60 Minutes*, Morley Safer asked May, his adopted mom, how Leslie could do what he does. May said, "Well, I think because the brain was damaged, a part of the brain—the musical part—God left perfectly healthy and beautiful so Leslie could have a talent. And he got it!"

Dr. Sacks also wrote about another person with autism who had similar intellectual abilities, hydrocephalus, and seizures but who had remarkable unusual abilities:

He cannot tie his shoes, he cannot add three plus two, but he can play you a movement of a Beethoven symphony and can transpose it to any key. He seems to have a rich understanding of the "grammar" of conventional harmony. I have been having him listen to more complex harmonies (including Debussy, the Berg piano sonata, the opening of Tristan, and the Ligeti piano etudes), and he can improvise now using any of these harmonic "languages."... He has a tremendous love of music ... and when he is playing well (which is not always) his playing is extraordinarily beautiful and moving. [2]

The same author was introduced to another writer whose father had Alzheimer's for 13 years. This is was what she told Dr. Oliver Sacks:

The plaque has apparently invaded a large amount of his brain, and he can't remember much of anything about his life. However, he remembers the baritone part to almost every song he has ever sung. He has performed with a twelve-man acappella singing group for almost forty years ... Music is one of the only things that keep him grounded in this world. He has no idea what he did for a living, where he is living now, or what he did ten minutes ago. Almost every memory is gone ... except for the music. In fact, he

---

2 Sacks, Oliver, *Musicophilia* Chap.12 P 165

opened for the Radio City Music Hall Rockettes in Detroit
this past November ... the evening he performed, he had no
idea how to tie a tie ... he got lost on the way to the stage,
but the performance! Perfect ... he performed beautifully
and remembered all the parts and words.[3]

Probably the most famous savant is Kim Peek, whom Dustin Hoffman depicted in the 1988 movie *Rain Man.* I recall a radio documentary where Peek said he can read two pages in less than five seconds and can remember everything he's read. He has read thousands of books, and retains the memory of all of them.

In the *Huffington Post,* I read about Stephen Wilshire who was diagnosed with severe autism at the age of three. He is a "human camera" who can draw vivid, detailed buildings and paint skylines of entire cities, such as Tokyo, Hong Kong, Frankfort, Madrid, Dubai, Jerusalem, and London with only a short visual visit. You can even watch a live-stream of Stephen drawing the cityscape of New York on the Internet.[4]

During a December 9, 2010 ABC interview, a 31 year old with Asperger's named Daniel Tammet said, "Children would tease me. I would have gestures ... flapping of the hands, walking in circles." The children who made fun of him had no idea that he would become one of the greatest mathematicians in the history of the human race!

According to the interview, "He is a mathematical genius, capable of astronomical calculations in the blink of an eye; and is a gifted linguist, speaking nine languages, including one he created called *Manti.*"

Daniel doesn't require a calculator and has Synesthesia, which occurs when regions of the brain associated with different abilities are able to form unusual connections, for example, secondary sensations of sound as color or of color as sound. It is my understanding that the average person with autism has rather immature short-range connections and fewer mature long-range connections between the two sides of the brain. Basically, the right and left hemispheres of the brain are less connected in those with autism. According to the ABC News website, "In most people's brains, the recognition of colors, the ability to manipulate numbers, or the capacity to understand language all work differently in separate parts of the brain, and the information is generally kept divided to prevent information

---

3　Ibid. p. 374 and 375
4　www.huffingtonpost.com/2009/.../autistic-artist-stephen-w_n_334703.html

overload. But in synesthetes, the brain communicates between the regions."[5]

Dr. Robert Melillo in his book, *Autism*, shares his theory regarding savant syndrome.

When we look inside the autistic brain, we can see that something abnormal is taking place. I, as well as many other experts, believe that certain environmental factors are turning off the expression of key genes involved in building the brains, which is interfering with normal development. As a result, certain areas of the brain, particularly on one side, are unable to communicate well with other areas of the brain and, in some children, are not communicating at all. This creates what we call functional disconnection syndrome (FDS), meaning certain areas and/or one side of the brain are either growing too fast or too slow relative to other areas, causing the two sides of the brain to get out of balance, which disrupts the communication between these areas. It is the only theory that can explain the unevenness of skills that are the hallmark of autism. It is why a child may be great at math but find reading difficult. It is why all children with autism appear drawn into their own world and are challenged in the area of social skills. It is why children with autism commonly are fixated on repetitive tasks, such as counting, or repetitive movements, such as arm flapping. The extreme example of this unevenness of skills is the rare individual who displays seemingly superhuman exceptional abilities in one area, but is extremely impaired in others— what we call savant syndrome.[6]

In theosophy and anthroposophy, there is a theory that all knowledge, events and experiences are encoded in a non-physical plane of existence referred to as the astral plane. Could there be an inner dimension of consciousness that records the vibrational journey and ideas of every person that has ever consciously existed? Let us imagine enlarging the current virtual World Wide Web to a real universal cosmic wide web where all previous knowledge and wisdom exists in an eternal quantum field. For the purpose of this conversation, let us refer to this possible analogy as the "inner-net."

---

5 ABC News, May 28, 2010, Nick Watt interview with Daniel Tammet, http://abcnews.go.com/2020/autistic-savant-daniel-tammet-solves-problems-blink-eye/story?id=10759598
6 Melillo, Robert, *Autism* New York(Penguin Group January 2013) Chap.3, P 35

Let us suppose a person with extraordinary gifts has the rare ability to tap into this inner-net and connect with specific genius resources. Could this also be the source of many inventions? I have heard that inventors such as Edison and Einstein received many of their ideas from dreams or intuition. Therefore, could this be the non-physical medium through which great artists, writers, and musicians receive their masterpieces? Is it possible that autistic savants like our aforementioned musical geniuses and mathematical wizard—because of their brain biology—are able to tap into this human inner-net to serve as great interpreters of music or human calculators? If so, just think of the extraordinary feats humankind may perform once the medical world truly understands the mysteries of the mind and brain!

CHAPTER 13

The Gifts of Service

Not only do people with autism and Alzheimer's have special gifts to share, but in their need of support and care, they touch billions of people worldwide.

I dedicate this chapter to my sister Gloria Routson-Gim-Belluardo, who took care of my mom, and to my niece Paula Routson-Jordan, who would drive nine hours just to attend a care meeting and to meet all of my mom's care providers.

Initially my book research was not without skepticism. My reaction was often "How do you see any gifts in autism?" And "There can't be anything positive about Alzheimer's!" Nevertheless, I felt an inspirational inner nudging, like divine intervention that inspired me to continue.

One morning, I went to breakfast and in the magazine I was reading was an article about the gifts of neurodiversity by Thomas Armstrong, and it referred to the gifts of autism. A second outside validation that I was on course was in a used bookstore, where John Zeisel's book, *I'm Still Here*, fell off the shelf and hit me on the head. Without knowing the title of the last chapter, I emailed John, and when he responded the same day, I was elated when after reading his email, I opened his book to chapter 10: "The Gifts of Alzheimer's: Insights from Learning to Give and Receive." In this chapter, he shares stories of caretakers of persons with Alzheimer's and personal gifts they feel they received in doing so. Dr. Zeisel conveys solace in his wise words when he explains that there is life after an Alzheimer's diagnosis for both the person diagnosed and their families and caretakers:

> But there is more that can be positive in a life with Alzheimer's. Being present to someone living with the illness teaches profound, usually unspoken, and often surprising lessons to those open to change. For them, it is as if the relationships foster and unwrap special personal "gifts" in the developing relationship. In relationship with people living with Alzheimer's we learn a great deal both about them and about ourselves.[1]

---

1 Zeisel, John, *I'm Still Here: A New Philosophy of Alzheimer's Care*, (New York, NY: Penguin Group, 2010), p. 217.

These gifts are a sense of purpose, gaining opportunities to serve, empower, uplift, nurture, and love unconditionally, and to assist in creating as much quality of life as possible.

Early in my career, I developed and co-coordinated a foster care program in Dayton, Ohio. The first provider I met was a woman who grew up in a children's home in Dallas. "More than anything else, I wanted a family," she said. Her longing to love and to nurture prompted her to marry at 18 and to have as many children as she could manage. For more than a dozen years, she lived on a farm with her minister husband and growing family. However, in 1969, an accident wiped out her family in one fell swoop. Her husband, four sons, and a daughter died when their car collided with a train. She spent months in a Dallas hospital. She wandered from place to place "I guess I was looking for a reason to go on living." She spent the rest of her life providing a living and nurturing home to two people with disabilities.

I had the privilege and pleasure of meeting so many staff working in assisted living and nursing homes who had dedicated their lives to taking care of people like my mom.

One of them was Maria Severt, who cared for my mother and said on her Facebook page:

The things I would do for one more day with this woman! One of the most amazing beautiful spirits, loving heart I have ever met. I miss you and think of you every day, Fern Routson! That year I got to spend with you was truly the best! I looked forward to going to work. You were my escape from all the wrong going on in my life, you always put a smile on my face, and you inspired me to love my job and reassured me that this was the career for me. I am so glad you were able to hold Miley the day you went to be with Jesus. I love you Fern, and I will see you again someday!

Patience to work with her, the belief that she was better off than us because she has no stress or worry. Fern and her condition helped me look at life and knowledge as a gift because we do not have forever.

I will also be forever grateful for the gift of love my mom, siblings, and I received when the Borchers family provided my mother with a loving, happy home. Mom broke her hip and had to move from an assisted living to a nursing home. The difference between the nursing home and the Borcher's family farm is a great example of "behavior is language" and the power of love! Mom appeared to be starting her last stages of Alzheimer's while at the nursing home, refusing to eat, becoming withdrawn and depressed. I believe these behaviors appeared because of unkind staff.

The Borchers family agreed to care for my mom when my sister told them that she literally escaped from the nursing facility in her wheelchair on a cold snowy February day. Only after a month at the farm, Mom not only regained her appetite, but also her functioning capacity returned to where she had been several years prior. She would laugh, smile, and sing and was once more a happy girl.

Lucy Borchers, my mother's main caregiver, said, "Taking care of Fern was a gift of love by assisting her to live and enjoy each day. It was a gift just to watch her feed 'her baby' and shower it with love and affection. It was a privilege taking care of her because I loved Fern and her family."

Lucy's daughter Hanna said, "Fern taught me patience, to be delicate because that is the way she needed to be cared for. Even though she was a little difficult at times, she brightened up my day by some of the simplest things. Fern really didn't know what she was saying often times, but it made an impact on me in many ways. Fern was one of the sweetest women I have taken care of!"

As I have mentioned, I am a huge believer in the work of Peter J. Whitehouse, M.D., Ph.D and love his book, *The Myths of Alzheimer's*:

> Having a sense of purpose in life and a sense of belonging to a family and community is also critical to individual well-being. If physicians spend all their time talking about drugs, there is little time to discuss other life options that may contribute to preserving and even enhancing quality of life."[2]

Besides making readers aware of alternatives to medicine and traditional treatment for dementia, *The Myths of Alzheimer's* also discusses the importance of volunteering and being active in the community. One of the many things that impressed me about Dr. Whitehouse was his involvement with his wife Cathy in the development of the world's first intergenerational charter schools (www.tisonline.org), which are free, high-performing public charter schools in Cleveland, Ohio, whose model revolves around including older adults as an intentional educational design element.

---

2 Whitehouse, Peter, *The Myths of Alzheimer's* (New York, NY: St. Martin's Press, 2008), p. 147.

Such a school would have been ideal for my mom. Her number-one passion in life was children, and she loved to read aloud. Even after she lost many of her skills, my mom loved reading aloud to us—anything she could get her hands on, but especially newspapers.

About his educational model, Dr. Whitehouse says:

> *In addition to reading, our other intergenerational programs focus on the use of computers, gardening, and other activities designed to stimulate the bodies and minds of learners of all ages, and create opportunities for the mutual transfer of knowledge and wisdom. Gardening allows learners of all ages to learn about natural cycles, food production, and the enjoyment of natural settings. In the Intergenerational School, we are demonstrating that a different model of public education can provide not only better learning for children, but can also create opportunities for older adults to contribute in a purposeful way to the future of their communities, share their collective wisdom, and stay cognitively vital in the process.* [3]

Such volunteering can also provide an opportunity to empower people with dementia and other disabilities while giving the volunteers a purpose. Gifts for all!

I believe that the spiritual synchronicities that attracted to me these books which were instrumental to my research were likewise instrumental in saving my life by leading me to my fulfilling career.

Going from an all-black school high school to attend an all-white high school for my junior and senior years presented me with challenges, particularly with being bullied. To overcome the bullying and my massive inferiority complex, I started drinking heavily and hanging out with the wrong crowd. I graduated from high school with a low self-esteem, and tried to sooth myself and fill my void with alcohol, but I also understood the pull for my time in nature. Despite my reliance on alcohol, nature helped empower me and began putting me in touch with my inner spiritual self.

Shortly after high school, I began reading self-help books such as Norman Vincent Peale's *The Power of Positive Thinking*. About a year after graduating high school, I believe spirit led me to an institution for severely disabled children, where I encountered children who were more deformed beyond anything I had even heard of. I never knew about conditions such as hydrocephalus (water on the brain)

---

3   Ibid., p. 146

that caused children to have heads as flat as pancakes because they were unable to move and reposition themselves, or that children could be born without faces, requiring tube feeding. One eight-year-old child with hydrocephalus, whom I remember particularly, had a head larger than his body, requiring him to live upside-down and use his hands to support his body as he used his feet like hands. In fact, this boy was so capable with his feet, that he used them better than most of the residents could use their hands!

I began volunteering several days a week helping to dress, bath, and feed the residents. I quickly fell in love with those children, and it soon became my purpose to thrive. Seeing that most of these children spent there entire life in their beds, I decided to start an educational and therapy program with the volunteer staff, for which the physical therapist would visit to teach me and the other volunteers to do range-of-motion exercises with the residents. I started to volunteer every day, up to 70 hours a week.

How empowering and rewarding it was, after months of trying to teach a child how to sit and bring a spoonful of food to their mouth, to actually see them succeed!

Finally, I had a purpose to my life. These children gave me the gift of service that filled the void I had been experiencing. My growing sense of purpose and accomplishment, in tandem with the enrichment and empowerment of self that I was learning from my various self-help books helped me to no longer need alcohol.

From that time forward, I learned that when you love and believe in yourself and consciously connect socially, emotionally, and spiritually—what a combination!

At this time in my life, I began to realize that when I had such a spiritual connection to myself and others, the little synchronicities would themselves become more common. I worked with a volunteer at the time—Sarah Herner—whose husband called me and said that Sarah had told him about my work and that he knew of a paying job that I may be interested in. John Herner was one of the early pioneers in the advocacy and passage of Public Law 94-142 Education of All Handicapped Children Act, which assured all children the right to an education no matter their disability. John was the director of the regional program for disabilities, and would later become the Superintendent of Education for the state of Ohio and also President of the National Association of State Directors of Special Education. That telephone call from John was indeed an affirmative sign that it launched my 40-year-plus joy-filled, illustrious career!

This gift of service was also the beginning of my lessons in understanding the power of appreciation and gratitude and also the

FINAL THOUGHTS

Ken Routson
Little did I know when I started this journey to focus on the gifts of autism and Alzheimer's that I would explore the mind, body, and spirit in association with Alzheimer's and the genetics of autism. Although I still have questions to research, I do believe there is a connection between stress and autism, as I said in a previous chapter, and I am certain stress is a major factor in Alzheimer's.

The more I reflect on Mom's life after reading the work of Dr. Gabor Maté, I see that she was the embodiment of his illustrations, especially with regard to her long-term chronic stress and repressed emotions and their effect on her autoimmune system.

In 1992, Mom opened up to a reporter during a period when my sister Cherie was in a coma, about her life as a child in rural eastern Ohio. When her mother died when she was a child, she and her father lived alone, and when she crossed him, he beat her with a razor strap, leaving welts over her body. "I told him I would stand there and take it," she said, "as long as he didn't hit me in the face." In this front-page article, the reporter told the story that once she cried out in pain when her father's dull clippers chewed and cut her skin during a haircut. "He got so mad," she said, that "he cut off every bit of my hair."

I am sure her father, my grandfather, was abused at some point as well, leading to this multi-generational stress pattern. Mom learned as child, I suppose, how to repress her pain and anger, which then began to suppress her immune system such that it eventually turned on her. I believe the autoimmune issues also became the source of her other illnesses. I thought of Dr. Mate's case studies about people with rheumatoid arthritis and irritable bowel disease, and how Mom was a young adult when her finger and hands became disfigured. My mom was also a chronic worrier and suffered with irritable bowel syndrome (IBS). I myself am a recovering worrier with a long history of IBS.

Mom had few friends and was extremely emotionally dependent on her children, so I believe that facing a life without a husband and then "losing control" of her children and finances all intensified the stress and illness-inducing toxic hormones.

So I have wondered: do all of those who experience chronic stress without a good stress response system have a propensity to have children with autism or do they themselves necessarily become victims of Alzheimer's? If the good doctors I have quoted in this book are correct, then it depends significantly on *their response* to stress and life's challenges as well as genetic disposition.

If my mom had learned to use healthy anger to set boundaries and not to repress, suppress, and depress emotions—and allow herself to be angry when needed to be—would she have been less of a pressure cooker that would erupt into unhealthy rage? If Mom could have learned how to transform her childhood pain, hurt, guilt, and unworthiness into unconditional love and acceptance of self, could she have been able to become her authentic self? I think so.

Also in the newspaper article, a local psychologist named Phyllis Kuehnl was quoted about the effect of my mother's upbringing on my sister based on her experience with cases similar to my sister's:

> *The lack of love and joy in Fern's life made it difficult for her to express affection, Kuehnl said. And the loss of her mother and abuse by her father left her unable to deal with adult stresses.*

> *Though Fern later became a better parent, Cherie—her eldest—bore the brunt of her frustration. And with all her emotional baggage, Fern Routson was on her own. Psychologists, therapists, counselors, and self-help books wouldn't come for a decade. Too late for Cherie.*

Maybe we need to focus as much time, money, and other resources on researching what we are doing emotionally—or not doing—to make ourselves sick instead of focusing strictly on biological factors such as, in the case of Alzheimer's, plaques and tangles. We as individuals need to reclaim our power to become more assertive and confident and become our whole, authentic, balanced, peaceful selves by using both our right and left brains. We "healthy people" need to practice what we try to teach those with disabilities: to be self-determined.

When I finally completed my research and our book, Raun K. Kaufman sent me the manuscript for his forthcoming book *Autism Breakthrough: The Groundbreaking Method That Has Helped Families All Over the World* to review. One of the many things that impressed me was his statement, "I hear people complaining about false hope, but I never hear anyone worrying about false pessimism."

Finally, there are more people, books, agencies, methodologies and practices that are life affirming, person-centered that cultivates valued and self-empowered harmonious relationships! Along with Zeisel's book *I'm Still Here*, for those interested in progressive Alzheimer's care I highly recommend Raun K. Kaufman's new book *Autism Breakthrough*, for those of you who may be looking for an innovative approach to autism. Raun's own story of complete recovery from severe autism was recounted in the popular NBC-TV movie, *Son-Rise: A Miracle of Love* in 1979. Raun is now the Director of Global Education (and former CEO) of the Autism Treatment

Center of America™, the worldwide teaching center for The Son-Rise Program®—the same method that his parents developed to reach him.

Let's stop scaring ourselves to death by listening to the pharmaceutical commercials and other BEWARE! broadcasts. I say stress less, and express, experience, and enjoy more!

God, life, and the Universe are always supporting us if we get out of our own way. We need to learn how to say, "No more!" when we need to, stop trying to please others over ourselves, take more time for ourselves, and think for ourselves. How much healthier would our society be if young parents could teach their children to become more self-directed, self-reliant, believing in self, loving, and accepting of themselves and others unconditionally? My father lost his leg in his late 40s, had a stroke in his early 50s and died in his mid-50s. He never learned how to take time for himself. I believe most dis-ease is emotionally and stress based. I will spend the rest of my life doing life coaching, stress workshops, writing empowerment books and teaching others so they do not have to suffer needlessly like my family and so many others I have known.

I've always loved a picture my spiritual teacher had of a mother cat and her kittens relaxing with a caption below that read: "Relax in the ease and comfort or your own being." I believe that more people are realizing that our culture has become too focused on left-brain doing rather than allowing the right-brained drive toward relaxing—enjoying the art of just being!

Maybe we can learn from people with Alzheimer's and autism about being in the moment and how to say no—not always trying to please others. Most people with Alzheimer's autism are saying, "I am who I am. I am not going to change just because you are worried about what other people think!"

To answer one of the questions I asked you to ponder in Chapter 2, what if we thought of people with Alzheimer's and autism as *different*, not flawed? I especially feel that those people with Down syndrome or Asperger's are not accidents but have special unique gifts and purpose! What if these people with autism and Alzheimer's who are different are communicating in an evolved and expanded way ... beyond words? Once we realize that it is possible that these magnificent human beings have much to teach us, we can watch them for how we can be. They change our fundamental understanding of what communication is—of what it means to be human.

The next time you are with your favorite person who happens to have autism or Alzheimer's, give yourself a gift too. Take them out in nature and observe how it seems they are viewing everything for the very first time, like small children who are full of excitement and wonder! While you are with this person, take a moment yourself and "forget" about your to-do list and *feel* the stillness, equanimity, harmony, and bliss of just being in the beauty of the moment!

Lighten up! Laugh more! Worry less! (Judge and criticize *much* less.) Play more! Become less inhibited! Jump in the puddles! Take yourself and life less seriously!

Also, listen to your body for what it needs more than you listen to outside "authorities." If you don't enjoy working out or vigorous exercise, then choose a sport, opt to dance, take a yoga class, or just skip, run, or walk! Be moderate in all things. Spend more time with nature, your friends, and your loved ones. Enhance and cultivate your realization and partnership with God and trust that with that alliance, everything will work out for you. Let love, peace, and joy begin with you and radiate to your world! Make peace with what you cannot control. Be still and know that there is a spiritual and inspirational (in-spirit) gift in every situation even if it is something relating to autism or Alzheimer's!

"Flow, flow, flow yourself gently through your life ... merrily, merrily, merrily, merrily life is full of joy!"

Nancy Reder RN

When I was asked by my longtime friend Ken to co-author a book with him as a tribute to his mother who had experienced Alzheimer's, I was delighted and honored, but not without trepidation.

Yes, I had years of experience interacting with persons, both children and adults, with autism or Alzheimer's, but would my expertise be of value to those who either experience first-hand the disorders, or give care as a family member, caregiver, or service provider? Let alone the question of my writing skills!

I firmly believe, as Ken does, that persons with not only Alzheimer's and Autism, but all who have differences, give us gifts if we are in a position to recognize them. Yes, it can be extremely hard to perceive questionable gifts—often only time or hindsight may afford us such insights. If one does not come to that position of acceptance, he or she must have valid reasons.

We are all on our own journey, which is no less valuable, regardless of the circumstances or our skill level. The reality of what may be of value to one person may not be of value to another. Thus, I agreed to co-author this book, and my often inarticulate writing journey began. It has been an experience of a lifetime!

I am in my latter years, and looking back, I see I have been able to draw from all the joys and heartaches and successes and failures of a career that has helped make me the person I am today. The knowledge I have gained and the opportunities for empathy in gathering people's journeys has been exhilarating. I have been so honored and blessed.

Thank you to all who have been a part of this tribute to Ken's mother and the persons you have written about.

Armstrong, Thomas: *Neurodiversity*

Dispenza, Joe: *Breaking the Habit of Being Yourself*

Davidson, Ann: *Alzheimer: A Love Story*

D'Ambrosio, Richard Anthony: *No Language But a Cry*

Fleishman, Arthur: *Carly's Voice*

Grandin, Temple: *Thinking in Pictures*

Hay, Louise: *Heal Your Life*

Kaufman, Raun: *Autism Breakthrough*

Kitwood, Tom: *Dementia Reconsidered: The Person Comes First*

Isaacs, Paul: *Looking Through The Haze, The Autistic Spectrum*

Levine, Judith: *Do You Remember Me?*

Lipton, Bruce: *Biology of Belief*

Lipton, Bruce: *Spontaneous Evolution*

Mate, Gabor: *When the Body Says No*

Melillo, Robert: *Autism*

Neal, Mary MD: *To Heaven and Back*

Neill, A.S.: *Summerhill*

Potocny, Joseph: *Living with Alzheimer's*

Routson, Ken: *Beliefology*

Sacks, Oliver: *Musicophilia*

Stewart, Leslie: *Trust and Allow the Process of Life IN-JOY*

Stillman, William: *Autism and the God Connection*

Tammet, Daniel: *Born on a Blue Day*

Taylor, Jill: *My Stroke of Insight*

Whitehouse, Peter: *The Myth of Alzheimer's*

Zeisel, John: *I'm Still Here*

Zeisel, John : *Life Quality Alzheimer's Care in Assisted Living*

Brain Balance Center   www.brainbalancecenter.com

Video/Films
In My Language, Baggs, Amanda
Rainman, 1988 United Artists
Awakenings, Columbia Pictures
Son Rise, Columbia Pictures

Websites/Blogs
Hearthstone Alzheimers Care, www.thehearth.org
Artists for Alzheimers (ARTZ), www.artistsforalzheiners.org
Ellen Belk, Resources for Seniors, www.keepinmindinc.com
Barbara Worthington, Caregiver cards, www.caregivercards.biz/caregiver-cards
Alzheimer's Association, www.alz.org
Family Caregiver Alliance, www.caregiver.org
Gentle Teaching, www.positivelivingsupport.org
Joseph Potocny, http://living-with-alzhiemers.blogspot.com/

WORKSHOPS by Routson and Associates
- Sensitivity and Awareness Conflict Resolution and Enhancing Customer Service
- Behavior is Language
- Attitudes are Everything
- The Gifts of Alzheimer's, Autism, and Down syndrome
- Power of Music, Art and Theatre
- Empowerment of all regardless of disability or dis-ease
- Understanding Neurological disorders, neurodiversity, neuroplasticity and epigenetics
- Empowerment overcoming stress
- Transporting persons with disabilities
- Sensitivity/Awareness & Empowerment for Special Education Paraprofessionals
- Sexuality and developing healthy relationships regardless of disability

About The Authors

Ken Routson is an author, speaker, consultant, life coach, workshop facilitator and more. He is nationally recognized for his contributions in developing day programs and residential supports for people with disabilities, as well as for his popular sensitivity-training workshops for schools and social service agencies.

Ken has served as the CEO of several corporations, including a healthcare corporation that specializes in in-home support for people with severe disabilities.

Ken established some of the very first supported-living arrangements in Ohio, and the Butler County Board of DD therefore proclaimed him "Father of Supported Living in Butler County." For his work in assisting persons with severe disabilities in their moves from nursing homes to "real" homes with appropriate supports, Ken earned the "Pioneer Award" from the Ohio Head Injury Association.

Ken conducts life coaching sessions worldwide, based on his most popular book "Beliefology." He recently developed Routson and Associates, a consulting company and is often booked for speaking engagements, which he finds amazing considering he was born with speech aphasia and several other severe learning disabilities.

Nancy Reder RN, MSEd has enjoyed a 50-year career in medicine and disability services. Her experience in the field of disabilities includes working with both children and adults. She is a graduate of St. Rita's School of Nursing in Lima, Ohio; Central State University in Wilberforce, Ohio; and the University of Dayton in Dayton, Ohio. Nancy taught as Adjunct Professor at several local universities where she presented in-services focused on Developmental Disabilities. Since her retirement, she maintains her involvement in the disability field by volunteering to assist persons with special needs.

Nancy currently resides in Brookville, Ohio, with her husband Emmett, and two granddaughters, who fortunately live nearby.

Ken Routson and Nancy Reder are also available to speak at your event. Ken is also available for life coaching via telephone.

For further information and to order additional books:
www.giftsofautismandalzheimers.com
www.beliefology.com

513-594-5489
Tulip Press
P.O. Box 181212
Fairfield, Ohio 45018